INSIDE

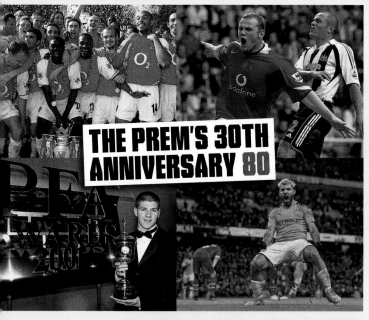

ENGLAND'S EPIC EUROS!

The Three Lions inspired the nation over the summer during their awesome European Championship adventure! MATCH looks back at their jaw-dropping journey...

SILLY STYLES!

Man. City midfielder Phil Foden only played 158 minutes at Euro 2020, but he had a massive impact on England fans - mainly because of his outrageous new hairstyle! He bleached his hair bright blond at the start of the tourno and started a new trend among Three Lions fans who decided to copy him!

AWESOME RECORDS!

England stars set some new records over the summer! Jordan Pickford didn't concede in his first five games to break a 55-year record for the most minutes without conceding by an England goalie, while Luke Shaw scored the fastest goal of a European Championship final with his strike against Italy in the second minute. Heroes!

HISTORY MAKERS!

Not only did Gareth Southgate's side end a 55-year jinx to beat Germany in the knockout rounds of a major tournament, they also made history by reaching the final of the European Championship for the first time in the nation's history - and reached their first major final since the 1966 World Cup!

WICKED WEMBLEY!

England played all but one of their Euro 2020 matches at their national stadium Wembley! Only 22,500 fans were allowed in to the famous ground for the group stage games, but that number gradually increased throughout the tournament until it reached its peak for the final with over 60,000 supporters inside. The atmosphere was absolutely electric!

SWEET CAROLINE!

Football's Coming Home will forever be the soundtrack to England fans' lives, but Sweet Caroline became the nation's unofficial anthem at Euro 2020! The players joined in with the sing-along after the victory v Denmark, while the song's writer, American Neil Diamond, said he now supports England too. So good, so good!

NOW TURN TO PAGE 66 FOR MATCH'S EURO 2020 SCRAPBOOK!

SOUTHGATE YOU'RE THE ONE!

The Three Lions are definitely in safe hands under Gareth Southgate! Here's why...

UNITY!

One of the things we've loved watching under Southgate is how together the squad seems! All of the players talk about how much they enjoy joining the camp, the club-like unity among them and how the gaffer is key to that!

VERSATILE!

Southgate has worked out a few different systems that England can play according to the opponent! The players know how to adapt to different formations, so they can change mid-game if they really need to!

YOUTH!

England's starting XI v Scotland had an average age of 25 years and 21 days - their youngest ever in a major tourno! Southgate has a great record of giving young players a chance, which is promising for the future!

TIGHT!

The Three Lions only conceded one goal from open play throughout the entire Euros and just six in eight games in qualifying for the tournament. They press from the front and defend as a team!

BRAVE!

Being England boss is one of the world's toughest jobs because every decision gets analysed! Southgate always sticks to his guns, though - like starting inexperienced CM Kalvin Phillips and using Kieran Trippier at left-back!

CHELSEA'S CLASS OF

4

1

2

3

1. CESAR AZPILICUETA

No player made more tackles in the 2020-21 Champions League than 'Dave' and the fan favourite also made history by becoming the first Spanish player to lift the Champions League as captain of a non-Spanish club! He's now won the CL, Europa League, Premier League, EFL Cup and FA Cup for Chelsea!

2. N'GOLO KANTE

The human battery made more ball recoveries and won more duels than any other player on the pitch – he was everywhere against City! He also became just the second player, after Pedro, to win the Champions League, Premier League, Europa League and World Cup!

3. REECE JAMES

The England wing-back made more tackles and more clearances than any other player on the pitch in the final against City! BT Sport pundit and former Champions League winner Rio Ferdinand reckons it was the game that turned the right-back into a man!

007 SHARP SHOOTER!

If Time To Die was Daniel Craig's last James Bond movie, we reckon Hollywood should look to Robert Lewandowski next – the lethal striker always hits the target!

FREESTYLE FUCHS!

Ex-Leicester ace *Christian Fuchs* can pull off around 20 Around The Worlds in a row, according to world champion footy freestyler *Andrew Henderson!* Who said defenders can't ball?

KING COMAN!

After winning the 2020-21 Bundesliga title with Bayern, winger Kingsley Coman has won ten league titles in a row – a 100% record since he became a professional!

2021!

6. KAI HAVERTZ

The German talent and match winner became the first star to score his first-ever Champions League goal in a final since 2021 opponent Ilkay Gundogan in 2013! He also became the youngest German player to score in a CL final since Borussia Dortmund's Lars Ricken in 1997!

5. EDOUARD MENDY

Mendy's nine clean sheets for Chelsea in the 2020-21 season is the most ever by a goalkeeper in their debut campaign in the competition! The wall also became the first African goalie to play in a Champions League final and the first since 1985 – when it was still known as the old European Cup!

4. THIAGO SILVA

The defender became Chelsea's oldest player to appear in a major European final at 36 years and 249 days old, overtaking former Blues midfielder Claude Makelele! He also became the fifth player to appear in the CL final in consecutive seasons but with different teams!

TURN TO PAGE 28 NOW TO READ ABOUT THE BEST CL XIS IN HISTORY!

GOALSCORING GOALKEEPERS!

Alisson's winner v West Brom in 2021 made him the sixth keeper to score a goal in Prem history, and the first with a header! Here are the others!

ASMIR BEGOVIC
November 2013

STOKE 1-1 SOUTHAMPTON

The quickest-ever goal from a keeper came after just 13 seconds when Begovic smashed a clearance over Artur Boruc's head!

TIM HOWARD
January 2012

EVERTON 1-2 BOLTON

Freak winds and a bonkers bounce saw USA keeper Howard score from 101 yards out, but he was too embarrassed to celebrate!

PAUL ROBINSON
March 2007

TOTTENHAM 3-1 WATFORD

The former England goalkeeper scored a crazy free-kick from 80 yards out, after the ball bounced over a helpless Ben Foster!

BRAD FRIEDEL
February 2004

CHARLTON 3-2 BLACKBURN

American shot-stopper Friedel fired a striker's finish from a stoppage-time corner, only to concede just moments later. Gutting!

PETER SCHMEICHEL
October 2001

EVERTON 3-2 ASTON VILLA

The first-ever Prem GK goal was a stunning volley at the back post from Kasper's dad, who went on to score an amazing 11 career goals!

DO YOU KNOW?

By winning the 2021 Championship play-off final against Swansea, Brentford have become the 50th club to feature in the Premier League! Can you name the other 49?

AWAY ADVANTAGE?

There were an incredible 153 away wins in the Premier League in 2020-21 compared to 144 home wins, making it the first season in Prem history that away victories outnumbered home victories!

COLD FEET!

Arsenal superstar Lia Walti has an interesting pre-match routine! She gets really cold before a game, so always heats her feet up with a hairdryer before putting her boots on!

ERLING HAALAND

SHATTERING RECORDS!

Ever since he burst onto the scene as a devastating teenage talent, Erling Braut Haaland has been breaking goalscoring records left, right and centre! We've picked out some of the best ones...

25

He scored 25 goals in his first 25 Bundesliga games! Nobody had ever done that before him, and we can't see anybody doing it in the future either!

6

It didn't take Haaland long to make an impact at international level. He scored six goals in his first six games for Norway, including a devastating hat-trick against Romania!

FIRST 20 EUROPEAN GAMES

Nobody's ever made such a strong start to life in Europe's club comps. Haaland scored 24 goals in his first 20 games - to give you an idea of how good this is, just see how it compares to Europe's other top goal grabbers!

PLAYER	GOALS
Erling Haaland	24
Kylian Mbappe	12
Lionel Messi	8
Robert Lewandowski	6
Cristiano Ronaldo	1

86

In three seasons at Red Bull Salzburg and Dortmund, he scored 86 goals in 86 games in all comps! He practically finds the net every time he steps onto the pitch!

WORLD CUP GOAL KINGS!

In 2021, Portugal's Cristiano Ronaldo became the all-time top scorer at the Men's European Championship – but who holds the World Cup record?

16

MIROSLAV KLOSE
Germany

15

RONALDO
Brazil

59

That's how many minutes it took Haaland to score his first five Bundesliga goals! He bagged a hat-trick off the bench on his Dortmund debut, then got two more on his next sub appearance a week later. That was enough to win him the Player of the Month, even though he'd played less than an hour!

10

In 2020-21, Haaland topped the Champions League scoring charts with ten goals – he's the youngest player in the competition's history to win the Golden Boot!

WHAT'S NEXT?

Haaland will have his eye on these records in 2021–22...

6	41	50	64
The record for Bundesliga goals in one game is six. Haaland bagged four in one game against Hertha Berlin in 2020 – can he go two better?	Robert Lewandowski set a new Bundesliga record for goals in a single season in 2020-21, but Haaland can beat it!	Haaland only needs to score ten times in the league to reach 50 Bundesliga goals! So far he's smashed home 40 goals in just 43 games!	If he reaches that landmark, he'll probably be the quickest player to hit that milestone too – Lewa holds the curent record at 64 games!

FOOTY'S BIGGEST BROMANCES!

MATCH reveals the best buds in the world of football...

DECLAN RICE & MASON MOUNT

These two have known each other ever since joining Chelsea's youth ranks as kids – no wonder they link up so well for England!

JESSE LINGARD & MARCUS RASHFORD

From busting out dance moves to dishing out LOL nicknames, their friendship dates back to their academy days at Man. United!

NEYMAR & DANI ALVES

The Brazilians first became friends on international duty when Neymar was a teen, and since then they've won trophies at Barca and PSG together!

EDEN HAZARD & THIBAUT COURTOIS

From playing with each other at Chelsea to Belgium and now Real Madrid, it seems wherever one goes the other will follow!

LIONEL MESSI & LUIS SUAREZ

During their time together at Barca, they formed a sick partnership and an unreal friendship. Leo was gutted when Suarez left the Nou Camp!

Stats correct up to the start of the 2021-22 season.

4

ERD MULLER
ermany

13

JUST FONTAINE
France

12

PELE
Brazil

WOMEN'S Euro 2022!

The summer of 2022 is another big one for England, as the nation prepares to host the postponed Women's European Championship! Here's the lowdown...

THE HOSTS!

England were supposed to host the Women's Euros in 2021, but it was postponed a year so it didn't clash with the men's tournament, which was also hosting games! The last time England hosted the women's competition, in 2005, The Lionesses got dumped out in the groups, so they'll be hoping to do much better in 2022!

THE EVENT!

The 2022 edition in England promises to be the biggest women's football event in history, with extensive coverage of all 31 matches to feature on free-to-air television, radio and online! The opening match will take place at Old Trafford and the final will be held at Wembley, while there will also be VAR in place for the first time ever at the Women's Euros!

THE HOLDERS!

The 2017 Euros was the first to feature 16 nations, expanded from 12 from the previous edition! It was hosted by the Netherlands - and actually won by the Netherlands! They lifted the trophy for the first time in their history after beating Denmark 4-2 in the final, ending Germany's 22-year reign as champions of Europe!

THE NEWBIES!

Of the 16 countries to have qualified for the competition, only one will be making their Women's European Championship debut - Northern Ireland! The home nation were ranked 32nd out of 48 contenders before qualifying, but finished second in Group C and then thrashed Ukraine 4-1 on aggregate in the play-offs. Epic!

WORLD CUP 2022!

We've also got the Men's World Cup to look forward to in 2022!

THE HOSTS!

Qatar are hosting their first-ever World Cup and just the second-ever to be held entirely in Asia after the 2002 event in South Korea & Japan!

THE HOLDERS!

France are the holders after winning the 2018 eve in Russia! Kylian Mbappe and co. will be desperat to keep hold of their crown as world champions

THE STADIUMS!

1 Man. City Academy Stadium	**1** Leigh Sports Village Stadium	**1** Old Trafford	**2** New York Stadium	**3** Bramall Lane

Here are the ten host stadiums for all the action!

UEFA women's EURO
ENGLAND 2022

4 Stadium MK	**5** Brentford Community Stadium	**5** Wembley Stadium	**6** St. Mary's Stadium	**7** Amex Stadium

---

GUESS THE TWEETER!

Match the footballers, past and present, to their hilarious tweets!

1 MICHAEL OWEN

A — I HAD SPAGHETTI AND IT WAS VERY NICE I ENJOYED IT

2 VICTOR WANYAMA

B — JUST TO CONFIRM TO ALL MY FOLLOWERS I HAVE HAD A HAIR TRANSPLANT. I WAS GOING BALD AT 25 WHY NOT.

3 ROBERT HUTH

C — WATCHED MY EIGHTH EVER FILM ON THE FLIGHT HERE. MUST HAVE BEEN BORED. #HATEFILMS

4 ROMELU LUKAKU

D — THANK YOU HOMER SIMPSON FOR COMING TO WATCH MY GAME AND CHEERING ME ON

5 DELE ALLI

E — I HATE CHRISTMAS.

6 ALLAN SAINT-MAXIMIN

F — JUST HAD SOME KIDS DOING TRICK OR TREAT AT MY DOOR... IT'S THE FIRST TIME IT HAPPENED IN MY LIFE HAHA

7 WAYNE ROONEY

G — MICROSOFT BOUGHT SKYPE FOR 8.5 MILLION DOLLARS. LOL IDIOTS! THEY COULD HAVE DOWNLOADED IT FOR FREE!

THE VENUES!

As part of their bid, Qatar promised to build eight new stadiums for the event, all equipped with cooling that can reduce the temperatures by up to 20C!

THE EVENT!

Due to the intense summer heat, the 2022 World Cup will be held from late November to mid-December, making it the first to be held in those months!

THE LOGO!

The official emblem not only resembles the trophy, but also the number 8 for the eight grounds, while the waves are supposed to represent desert dunes!

Answers: 1C; 2A; 3E; 4F; 5G; 6D; 7B.

MATCH! **11**

WIN PRIZES!

£250 RASCAL VOUCHER!

CLOSING DATE: JAN. 31 2022

Thanks to our massive mates at Rascal Clothing, we're giving away a £250 voucher to spend on their website! Imagine all the epic gear you could land with that...

Rascal Clothing is an active lifestyle brand, fronted by F2 Freestylers Billy Wingrove and Jeremy Lynch!

Rascal Clothing prioritises movement, style and comfort for every seasonal fashion collection!

You can check out the full range of Rascal gear at rascalclothing.com and follow them and the F2 on social media @rascal_clothing and @theF2

HOW TO ENTER! ➤ WWW.MATCHFOOTBALL.CO.UK

Then click 'Win' in the navigation bar on the MATCH website. Full T&Cs are available online.

MATCH!
THE BEST FOOTBALL MAGAZINE!

SON HEUNG-MIN

ANSWERS ON PAGE 94 ▶▶

1 True or False? The 2019 Ballon d'Or nominee was the first player from Asia to score 0 goals in the Prem!

2 Which German team did Tottenham sign him from - Wolfsburg, Bayern Munich, Schalke or Bayer Leverkusen?

3 He won the 2020 FIFA Puskas Award after netting a solo goal in the Prem against who - Burnley or Brighton?

4 Did the South Korea legend score his first goal for Tottenham in the Premier League or Europa League?

5 True or False? The lightning-quick goal grabber helped South Korea win gold at the 2018 Asian Games!

2022'S A BIG YEAR FOR...
GREALISH

Can the Man. City man deliver after his record-breaking transfer?

THE STORY SO FAR...

After making his Aston Villa debut in 2012, Grealish saw some mega highs and huge lows at his boyhood club! An FA Cup final, relegation, play-off heartbreak and promotion was all packed in before he established himself as a real Prem star!

In 2020-21, Grealish went from being not just Villa's best player, but one of the hottest properties in the Prem! His flair helped him bag six goals and ten assists, and he would've got tons more if it wasn't for injury in the second half of the season!

Grealish went to Euro 2020 with tons of hype from the fans as one of England's most exciting attacking stars! Shortly after The Three Lions' final defeat, he became the most expensive British player ever – joining Man. City for £100 million!

AWESOME ATTACK!

Most of the footballing world's eyes will be on Paris in 2021-22 to see Kylian Mbappe, Neymar and Lionel Messi in action, but we reckon Man. City's new-look attack could be just as good! If Grealish clicks with his England pals Raheem Sterling and Phil Foden, backed up by Kevin De Bruyne's creativity, the Prem champs could rack up a record-breaking number of goals!

NO MORE WEMBLEY HEARTBREAK?

Before joining City, Grealish had lost four Wembley finals – the 2015 FA Cup, 2019 EFL Cup, Euro 2020 and 2018 play-offs! His first appearance for his new club was in the Community Shield against Leicester and guess what... he lost again! Next time Jack plays at the national stadium he'll want to walk off with a winners' medal!

MANCHESTER CITY

TASTE OF EUROPE!

Grealish's monster move means that he'll get to play European football for the first time in his career and, by the time 2022 begins, City should be looking ahead to the Champions League knockout stages! Last season they were beaten in the final by Chelsea but, after splashing out so big on Grealish, they'll be hoping he can take them all the way this time!

WORLD CUP STARTER?

Although Grealish played a part in England's incredible Euro 2020 journey, he only started once, with all his other appearances coming off the substitutes' bench. By the time the World Cup rolls around in Qatar, he'll want to be one of Gareth Southgate's first-choice starters, and if he's racking up goals and assists for Man. City he'll be impossible to ignore!

2022 IN NUMBERS...

10
Jack's stepping into huge shoes by taking Sergio Aguero's No.10 shirt! Can he deliver epic moments like the legendary Argentina striker?

1
Grealish is yet to win a first major trophy in his career, but he's at the perfect club to end that wait!

0
At the start of the 2021-22 season he was still waiting for his first England goal! How many will he have by the end of 2022?

8
His best-ever league scoring season was eight in 2019-20, but he has to bag more than that this year!

JUDE'S RIVALS

These elite teenage tyros could all be considered Europe's top wonderkid, too!

PEDRI

Age: 18 ★ Midfielder
Barcelona ★ Spain

Pedri was playing in the Spanish second division in 2020, but you wouldn't have known that watching him play at the Euros - he was one of the main men in Spain's midfield and even made the official Team of the Tournament! He put his stamp on the Barcelona team in his first season too, and could be a star at the Nou Camp for years to come!

TOP FIVE SKILLS

Skill	Rating
DRIBBLING	9
PASSING	10
VISION	9
TECHNIQUE	9

HE'S THE NEXT...
DAVID SILVA

MASON GREENWOOD

Age: 19 ★ Forward
Man. United ★ England

Greenwood was unlucky to be ruled out of Euro 2020 through injury, but he'll get plenty more chances in an England shirt. He's already a deadly finisher and has all the tools to become a world-class No.9 – plus he's got the perfect teacher in Man. United team-mate Edinson Cavani. We reckon the young hot-shot could score tons in 2022!

TOP FIVE SKILLS

Skill	Rating
FINISHING	9
SPEED	9
MOVEMENT	8
TECHNIQUE	8

HE'S THE NEXT...
EDINSON CAVANI

EDUARDO CAMAVINGA

Age: 18 ★ Midfielder
Real Madrid ★ France

As an incredible teenage sensation, Camavinga had already racked up over 80 professional games for Rennes across three seasons, including four in the Champions League! He's a total all-rounder, capable of bossing games from deep or getting up and down the pitch as a box-to-box beast - no wonder Real Madrid signed him!

TOP FIVE SKILLS

Skill	Rating
PASSING	9
TECHNIQUE	8
ENERGY	9
TACKLING	7

HE'S THE NEXT...
PAUL POGBA

ANSU FATI

Age: 18 ★ Winger
Barcelona ★ Spain

Fati should have been alongside Pedri in the Spain squad at Euro 2020 but, like Greenwood, got ruled out through injury. Barcelona used to worry big time about how they were going to replace Lionel Messi, but not any more – Fati is the youngest goalscorer in their history and Leo's heir apparent. We think he's got everything to succeed!

TOP FIVE SKILLS

DRIBBLING		9
SPEED		9
FLAIR		8
FINISHING		7

HE'S THE NEXT…
LIONEL MESSI

ONES TO WATCH!

These highly-rated wonderkids could also make a name for themselves in 2022...

FLORIAN WIRTZ

Age: 18 ★ Att. midfielder
B. Leverkusen ★ Germany

The Germany U21 starlet is already a key player for Bayer Leverkusen after bursting onto the Bundesliga scene in 2020!

RAYAN CHERKI

Age: 18 ★ Winger
Lyon ★ France

Gossips reckon clubs in Europe are already queuing up to sign the tricky winger, but Lyon have high hopes for him!

JAMAL MUSIALA

Age: 18 ★ Midfielder
Bayern Munich ★ Germany

The talented ex-Chelsea youth academy midfielder played for England at youth level before switching to Germany!

HARVEY ELLIOTT

Age: 18 ★ Winger
Liverpool ★ England

After tearing it up on loan at Blackburn in 2020-21, Elliott is ready to make his mark on the Premier League!

YOUSSOUFA MOUKOKO

Age: 16 ★ Striker
B. Dortmund ★ Germany

The Bundesliga's youngest-ever player has scored tons of goals and broken loads of records at youth level. Massive future!

GIOVANNI REYNA

Age: 18 ★ Att. midfielder
B. Dortmund ★ USA

Bellingham isn't the only teenage wonderkid tearing it up in Borussia Dortmund's midfield – Reyna is an absolute baller too! The American is more attacking, and sometimes plays off the wing where he chips in with goals and assists. Last summer he scored in USA's Nations League final victory over Mexico!

TOP FIVE SKILLS

DRIBBLING		8
CREATIVITY		8
PASSING		7
SHOOTING		7

HE'S THE NEXT…
CHRISTIAN PULISIC

MATCH'S...
Crystal Ball!

We've taken a look into our crystal ball to predict what could happen in 2022!

Mou's new movie!

After re-watching Tottenham's Amazon Prime documentary, a famous filmmaker approaches Jose Mourinho to star in his new Hollywood blockbuster! The Roma coach immediately leaves his managerial role and decides to become a full-time actor, working alongside Sylvester Stallone in a new boxing drama: The Wrestle One!

The Spurs curse!

After Tottenham blow a two-goal lead in the FA Cup final, chairman Daniel Levy hires a clairvoyant to find out what's going wrong at the club! They discover that the Spurs trophy cabinet is indeed cursed, and that the only way to solve the problem is to dispose of all their previous trophies – much to rival fans' delight!

European Super Team!

Although their European Super League idea was shot down in 2020-21, the bosses of the continent's top clubs once again decide to team up to form a new European Super Team! Two players are pinched from each squad to create a star-studded squad, but they lose their first friendly against Burnley U17s and withdraw through embarrassment!

Lingard breaks the Internet!

After scoring a tap-in in a pre-season friendly, Jesse Lingard breaks into a five-minute dance routine involving epic moonwalks, acrobatic flips and never-seen-before body movements! The cool clip instantly goes viral on social media, with over 10 million hits a second, causing a worldwide drop in the Internet for over a week!

Courteous Cristiano!

Portugal superstar Cristiano Ronaldo announces his plans to retire and offers an exclusive face-to-face interview with MATCH! He tells us how he plans to become a bus driver in Lisbon and, even more shockingly, how he intends to donate all his Ballon d'Or awards to who he rates as the greatest player in the history of football – Lionel Messi!

GRAHAM HAANSEN

ANSWERS ON PAGE 94 ▶▶

1 True or False? The tricky Norway winger scored a hat-trick on er debut for Barcelona gainst CD Tacon!

2 Which German team did Barca sign her from – Wolfsburg, Werder Bremen, Bayern Munich or Hoffenheim?

3 How many caps has she won for Norway since making her debut in 2011 – more than 80 or less than 80?

4 Which country has Graham Hansen not played club football in – Germany, Spain, Sweden or Italy?

5 Which awesome boot brand does the Barcelona goal king wear – Nike, adidas, Under Armour or Puma?

ICONIC

CLEAN PITS ONLY THOUGH, BRO!

THE SKY'S THE LIMIT!

PERFECT FOR TRICK OR TREATING, MATCH!

KYLIAN MBAPPE

'The Little Brother'

Celebration Difficulty: ★

Now that he's one of the biggest megastars in the world, it's only right that Mbappe's got his own trademark celebration! Even though we've seen him celebrate like this so many times since joining PSG, Kylian first started doing it at Monaco! He says it was first tested by his younger brother Ethan during some games on the PlayStation, and it's since been copied by the likes of Liverpool's Trent Alexander-Arnold!

Try It Out!

It'll make you look like an absolute boss and it's really easy to do, so it's definitely a celebration worth giving a go! Simply cross your arms on your chest and place your palms under the opposite armpit!

LAUTARO MARTINEZ

'The Crossed-Arms'

Celebration Difficulty: ★★

After netting tons of goals to help Inter win Serie A in 2020-21, Martinez was captured using tons of different celebrations throughout the season! However, it's crystal clear which one is his trademark! One of the cool things about his celebration is that – like Mbappe – he sometimes decides to do it standing up, and on other occasions he combines it with an epic knee slide. Quality!

Try It Out!

It's an easy celebration for you to pull out when you next score against your mates! All you have to do is cross your arms and make sure that both of your index fingers are pointing towards the sky!

MASON MOUNT

'The Frankenstein'

Celebration Difficulty: ★★★

If you're wondering where the midfielder got the idea for his hilarious 'Frankenstein' celebration, it was recommended to him by Internet personality Chunkz! Of course, as is the case with any dance move nowadays, it also went viral on TikTok with tons of influencers trying it out for themselves! Mount was even able to bust it out at Anfield after netting against Liverpool in 2020-21!

Try It Out!

If you fancy looking like 'Frankenstein' after scoring, then simply lift your hands up as if you're playing a keyboard and sway both of your knees from side to side at the same time! You'll find plenty of examples by taking a look on TikTok!

Easy

Celebrations!

SHAMONE!

HELP, I CAN'T SEE WHERE I'M GOING!

CRASH LANDING ALERT!

JESSE LINGARD

'The J-Lingz Dance'

Celebration Difficulty: ★★★

If the Premier League was a dancing contest, then there's no doubt that J-Lingz would come out on top every season! After scoring tons of goals on loan at West Ham in 2020-21, he's had plenty of opportunities to work out what his favourite move is! He's mainly inspired by the 'King of Pop' Michael Jackson, although we're still sure he makes some of his moves up on the spot!

Try It Out!

Why not give J-Lingz's moonwalk celebration a go? Start with one foot on the ball of the foot and have the other foot flat. Then, use the pressure on the floor to slide the flat foot back before switching feet. The faster you can do it, the cooler it looks!

STEVEN BERGWIJN

'The Finger Twist'

Celebration Difficulty: ★★★

We got a first glimpse of Bergwijn's trademark 'Finger Twist' after he netted on his debut for Spurs against Man. City in 2020! Even though he says the idea came from FIFA, Alexandre Pato has been caught celebrating in a similar fashion in the past! It's still the first time we've seen a celebration like it in the Premier League though, so we'll let the Dutchman take all the credit!

Try It Out!

It doesn't look too difficult to pull this one off, but it can actually be a little bit tricky to cross your middle finger if you're trying to do it at speed! Once you've managed to do that, all you have to do is use your hand to cover your face!

PIERRE-EMERICK AUBAMEYANG

'The Somersault'

Celebration Difficulty: ★★★★★

There's absolutely no doubt that the lightning-quick Gabon striker's forward somersault celebration is one of the craziest in the footy world! Whenever Auba nets, all of his team-mates make sure they stay well out of his way because they know what's coming next - some jaw-dropping acrobatics! He's had plenty of opportunities to perfect his technique over the last few years!

Try It Out!

Erm... actually, don't try this one at home unless you've got tons of experience in gymnastics! If you're still desperate to give it a go, then we'd recommend busting out a backflip in-game after scoring a screamer on FIFA instead!

Hard ➤➤➤➤➤➤

BIG MATCH! QUIZ

PREMIER LEAGUE SPECIAL

YouTube STAR!

Which Premier League hero has turned into FIFA YouTube icon KSI in this pic?

MATCH MATHS!

Work out the two numbers then add them together!

Times Pep Guardiola has won the Prem!	
Harry Maguire's Man. United shirt number!	
ANSWER	

FREAKY FACES!

Which Premier League striker has been given a bonkers makeover in this crazy pic?

THE NICKNAME GAME!

Match these Premier League clubs with their crazy nicknames!

Everton	Newcastle	Watford	Norwich
1	2	3	4
A	B	C	D
Magpies	Hornets	Canaries	Toffees

GROUNDED!

Can you name the cool ground where Wolves play their home games?

FOOTY MIS-MATCH

Spot the ten differences between these two Manchester derby pics from last season!

1
2
3
4
5

6
7
8
9
10

ANSWERS ON PAGE 94

STRIKERS WORDFIT!

Fit 30 past and present PL hitmen into the grid!

Abraham	Firmino	Richarlison
Adams	Giroud	Rodriguez
Antonio	Iheanacho	Silva
Aubameyang	Ings	Toney
Bamford	Jesus	Vardy
Barnes	Kane	Watkins
Batshuayi	Lacazette	Welbeck
Benteke	Nketiah	Werner
Calvert-Lewin	Pukki	Wilson
Cavani	Rashford	Wood

AUBAMEYANG

ANSWERS ON PAGE 94

BENZEMA

ANSWERS ON PAGE 94 ▶▶

1 True or False? The Real Madrid goal grabber plays for France, but he was actually born in Algeria!

2 In which year did the deadly striker sign for Spanish giants Real Madrid – 2009, 2010 or 2011?

3 How many league titles did he win with Lyon before moving to Spain – none, one, two, three or four?

4 Which team did he make his international debut against back in March 2007 – Italy, Greece, Austria or Switzerland?

5 True or False? Benzema was nicknamed Coco by his friends when he was younger!

CHAMPIONS LEAGUE STARTING XIs!

MATCH looks through the history books at some of the best-ever teams to win the Champions League trophy – without repeating the same club twice!

AC MILAN
2007

Dida

Oddo — Nesta — Maldini — Jankulovski

Gattuso — Pirlo — Ambrosini — Seedorf

Kaka — Inzaghi

THE FINAL!

Carlo Ancelotti's men had suffered the 'Miracle of Istanbul' in 2005, when they let a 3-0 lead slip against Liverpool in the CL final before losing on penalties! They got their revenge two years later, though – a Filippo Inzaghi brace helped Milan beat The Reds in Greece, despite Dirk Kuyt netting a late consolation!

WHY THEY ROCKED!

- They showed incredible courage, confidence and composure to put their demons of 2005 behind them!
- They defeated Bayern Munich at the Allianz Arena and Man. United in the semi-finals to reach the final!
- They had superstar talent all across the pitch, including Paolo Maldini, Andrea Pirlo, Clarence Seedorf and future Ballon d'Or winner Kaka!

AJAX
1995

Van der Sar

Reiziger — Blind — F. De Boer

Rijkaard

Seedorf — Litmanen — Davids

George — R. De Boer — Overmars

THE FINAL!

Ajax faced AC Milan back in 1995, with the Serie A side competing in their third consecutive CL final! A tight game in Vienna saw the deadlock broken in the 85th minute, with substitute Patrick Kluivert becoming the youngest player to score in a Champions League final aged just 18 years and 327 days old!

WHY THEY ROCKED!

- AC Milan were considered the strongest team in the world at the time, but Ajax beat them three times - including twice in the groups!
- They were a young team full of starlets like Kluivert, who would later go on to become household names!
- They played a silky, possession-based style of football that was easy on the eye and fun for the neutrals!

BARCELONA
2009

Valdes

Puyol — Toure — Pique — Sylvinho

Xavi — Busquets — Iniesta

Messi — Eto'o — Henry

THE FINAL!

Pep Guardiola's Barcelona met Man. United in the 2009 final at Rome's Stadio Olimpico! Samuel Eto'o opened the scoring in the tenth minute, before Leo Messi added another goal 20 minutes from the end to earn Barca a famous treble of La Liga, Copa del Rey and the Champions League!

WHY THEY ROCKED!

- They became the first-ever Spanish side to win the continental treble, writing their names into history!
- The legendary midfield trio of Andres Iniesta, Sergio Busquets and Xavi totally bossed possession!
- The front three was frightening! Thierry Henry and Messi were deadly off the wing, while Eto'o was a pacy striker with an eye for goal!

BAYERN MUNICH
2020

Neuer

Kimmich · Boateng · Alaba · Davies

Thiago · Goretzka

Gnabry · Muller · Coman

Lewandowski

WINNERS
UEFA CHAMPIONS LEAGUE 2019/20
CHAMPIONS

THE FINAL!

PSG and Bayern Munich played out the first-ever Champions Leauge final behind closed doors at the Estadio da Luz in Lisbon, with both sides eyeing up a continental treble! It ended up being a really tight game, but one that was eventually settled by ex-PSG winger Kingsley Coman's ace header!

WHY THEY ROCKED!

Bayern became the first-ever club to lift a European trophy with a 100% winning record. Total legends!

They became only the second European team in history to win the continental treble twice and ended the year with six trophies. Wowzers!

They were faultless all over the pitch – strong in defence, dominant in midfield and absolutely lethal up front!

BORUSSIA DORTMUND
1997

Klos

Reuter · Kohler · Sammer · Kree · Heinrich

Lambert · Sousa

Moller

Riedle · Chapuisat

THE FINAL!

Juventus were the holders of the trophy and heavy favourites going into the 1997 final against Borussia Dortmund, despite the match taking place in Germany! The game's largely remembered for wonderkid Lars Ricken's sensational lob just 16 seconds after coming on as a sub to seal the victory!

WHY THEY ROCKED!

Dortmund coach Ottmar Hitzfeld became only the second manager at the time to win the Champions League with two different clubs!

Ricken was a local boy who'd come through the club's academy, so his goal meant even more for the club!

Matthias Sammer was one of the very best sweepers in the history of footy and their rock at the back!

JUVENTUS
1996

Peruzzi

Torricelli · Ferrara · Vierchowod · Pessotto

Conte · Sousa · Deschamps

Ravanelli · Vialli · Del Piero

THE FINAL!

CL holders Ajax met Juventus in the 1996 final, with Juve desperate to put things right after missing out on the Serie A title to AC Milan! They went ahead after 13 minutes, only for Ajax to equalise before half-time. The game went to penalties, with the Italians holding their nerve to lift the tophy!

WHY THEY ROCKED!

They lost 1-0 in the quarter-final first leg v Real Madrid, but showed courage to win 2-0 in the second leg!

Playmaker Alessandro Del Piero scored in that comeback win and was the shining light of the team!

They were a typically well-drilled Italian side with midfielders Didier Deschamps, Paulo Sousa and Antonio Conte going on to become managers!

LIVERPOOL
2019

Alisson

Alexander-Arnold — Matip — Van Dijk — Robertson

Henderson — Fabinho — Wijnaldum

Salah — Firmino — Mane

THE FINAL!
The 2019 Champo League final was the seventh to feature two teams from the same country – Liverpool and Tottenham! Jurgen Klopp's Reds got off to a fast start, winning a penalty after just 106 seconds, which Mohamed Salah buried! Sub Divock Origi sealed the win late on to clinch the club's sixth CL crown!

WHY THEY ROCKED!
They showed stunning courage, spirit and motivation after losing the 2018 final to Real Madrid!

They totally outclassed German giants Bayern in the second leg of their last 16 knockout tie!

They pulled off one of the best comebacks in CL history in the semis – winning 4-0 against Barcelona at Anfield after losing the first leg 3-0!

MAN. UNITED
1999

Schmeichel

G. Neville — Johnsen — Stam — Irwin

Giggs — Beckham — Butt — Blomqvist

Yorke — Cole

THE FINAL!
The 1999 final between United and Bayern was of one of the most dramatic in history! Mario Basler put the Germans ahead after just six minutes, and they looked on course to lift the trophy with just stoppage-time left to play – only for Teddy Sheringham and Ole Gunnar Solskjaer to score two in two minutes!

WHY THEY ROCKED!
As well as their comeback in the final, they also turned a 3-1 deficit around v Juventus in the semi-finals!

They had to play the final without two key midfielders who were suspended – Roy Keane and Paul Scholes!

The CL capped off an incredible campaign where Alex Ferguson's side became the first English team to win the continental treble!

REAL MADRID
2018

Navas

Carvajal — Varane — Ramos — Marcelo

Modric — Casemiro — Kroos

Isco

Benzema — Ronaldo

THE FINAL!
After a tense and tight first half in Kiev, Real Madrid's clash with Liverpool exploded into life with four goals in the second half! Two of them were nightmare blunders from Reds goalkeeper Loris Karius, but Gareth Bale's stunning overhead kick was a moment of pure brilliance!

WHY THEY ROCKED!
They became the first team in the modern era of the Champo League to win three back-to-back trophies!

They had to defeat Juventus, PSG and Bayern Munich just to reach the final against Liverpool!

As well as Bale's mind-boggling overhead kick, Cristiano Ronaldo also scored one of his own acrobatic worldies in their knockout tie with Juve!

2022'S A BIG YEAR FOR...
SANCHO

Can Man. United's new winger take them back to the top?

THE STORY SO FAR...

Sancho has been tipped for greatness ever since he was a teenager! Man. City snapped him up from Watford when he was just 14 then, in 2017, he won Player of the Tournament at the Under-17 Euros! Europe was starting to take notice...

By the time he was 17, Sancho was pushing for first-team football. Although Man. City offered him a contract, he turned it down - choosing to join Borussia Dortmund instead for a bargain £8 million, and quickly became a key man for the Germans!

In four seasons in Germany, Sancho was one of the Bundesliga's most devastating attackers. He tore full-backs apart with his skills and dribbling, bagging 38 goals and 45 assists! That's why United chased him for so long and splashed out £73m to get him!

FUTURE NO.7?

Sancho will wear the No.25 shirt this season, but gossips say he'll inherit the No.7 sometime in the future - and there aren't many shirts in football as famous as Man. United's No.7! Superstars like George Best, Eric Cantona, David Beckham and Cristiano Ronaldo have all worn it, so Sancho will have massive boots to fill to add his name to that list of legends!

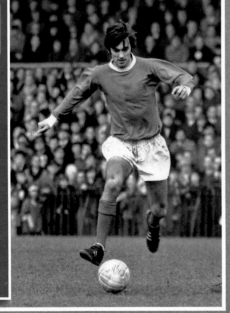

TRIPLE THREAT!

With Sancho linking up with Marcus Rashford and Mason Greenwood, The Red Devils will have an attack packed with pace, skill, flair and youth! The trio could potentially be tearing defences apart for years to come, and it's not just United fans that should be buzzing about that - Gareth Southgate would love to get that front three clicking in an England shirt, too!

WORLD CUP WIZARD!

Some England fans seemed to forget about Sancho while he was playing in Germany, but now that he's back in the Premier League he'll be hard to ignore. He had a heart-breaking time at the Euros - he only started one game, then missed a penalty in the final shootout against Italy - so he'll be desperate to make up for that in Qatar... as long as England qualify!

DERBY DAYS!

Although he left them without playing a single game, Man. City fans won't be happy seeing Sancho in a red shirt! He's in for a fierce reception when he rocks up at the Etihad for the first time in United colours in March, and it'll probably be one of the biggest tests of his career so far! If the winger can silence the hostile fans, it'll be a huge boost for him and his club!

2022 IN NUMBERS...

10
Sancho has bagged double figures for league assists for the last three seasons – can he achieve it in the Prem as well?

4
If he does, he'll match David Beckham's record of doing it four years in a row in one of Europe's top leagues. Hero!

2
In Qatar, Sancho will be eyeing his second World Cup winners' medal – he bagged one for the U17s in 2017!

5
2022 will mark five years since United last won a trophy! Can Sancho help end their wait?

Cristiano Ronaldo

When he isn't busy bamboozling defenders, C-Ron loves to hit the slopes!

Erling Haaland

Haaland says if he wasn't a footy megastar, he'd either be a rapper or a farmer!

Hector Bellerin

The full-back loves keeping up with the latest fashion trends, although we're not sure about those sandals!

HEROES' HOBBIES!

Sergio Aguero

The Argentina striker is one of the biggest gamers in the football world!

Jesse Lingard

J-Lingz loves keeping up with all the latest transfers just as much as MATCH!

Mohamed Salah

When he's in need of a bit of a cool down, Mo loves to have a dip!

Phil Foden

The City whizz-kid will be fishing for gold in all competitions with Pep Guardiola's men again this season!

MATCH can't get enough of seeing what these megastars get up to in their spare time!

Griezmann, Mbappe & Pogba

The France trio spent their spare time during Euro 2020 playing basketball! We'd love to know who did the most slam dunks!

Gareth Bale

The Welshman loves playing golf so much that he's even set up a course in his back garden!

Sergio Ramos

No wonder the rock-solid centre-back has such huge leg muscles – he spends all his spare time on his bike!

DESIGN A BOOT!

MATCH wants to branch out its epic merchandise by creating a new brand of football boots – and we need your help to design the very first pair!

SEND IT IN!

Send us a photo of your drawing and we'll feature the best ones in MATCH magazine and on our epic social media channels!

@ Email: match.magazine@kelsey.co.uk

f facebook.com/matchmagazine

🐦 twitter.com/matchmagazine

📷 instagram.com/matchmagofficial

BIG MATCH! QUIZ

CHAMPIONS LEAGUE SPECIAL

SWITCH!

Which Champions League striker has changed careers to become a Formula 1 driver?

5 QUESTIONS ON...

THE CHAMPIONS LEAGUE

1 True or False? Ancient football legend Zlatan Ibrahimovic has represented six different clubs in the competition!

2 Real Madrid have won the Champions League more than any team, but how many times have they bagged the trophy?

3 Which of these clubs didn't play in the Champions League in 2020-21 - Krasnodar, Midtjylland or Arsenal?

4 Who's scored more goals in the history of the Champions League - Lionel Messi, Cristiano Ronaldo or Robert Lewandowski?

5 Which amazing stadium will host the 2021-22 CL final - Wembley, the Allianz Arena, Nou Camp or Krestovsky Stadium?

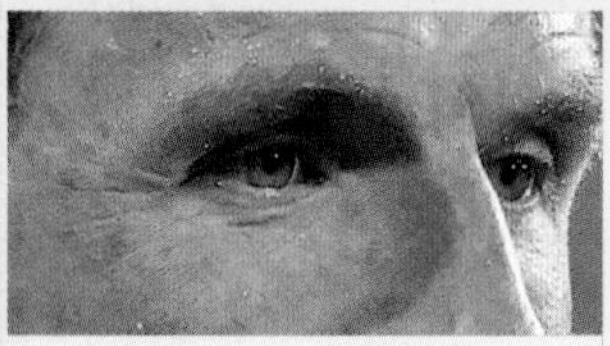

CLOSE-UP!

Which CL superstars have we zoomed in on here?

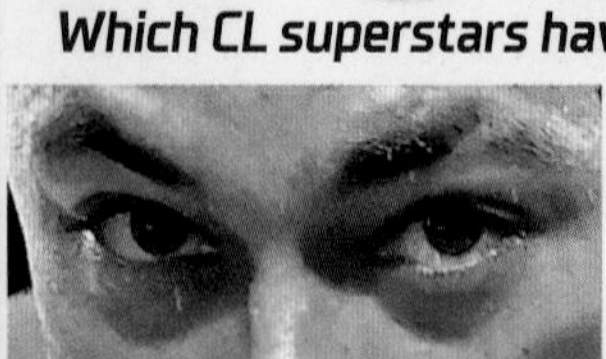

1.
2.
3.
4. 

SOCCER SCRABBLE

Rearrange these letters to figure out the name of a Champions League legend!

L D O R R N

N H O I

A

NAME THE TEAM!

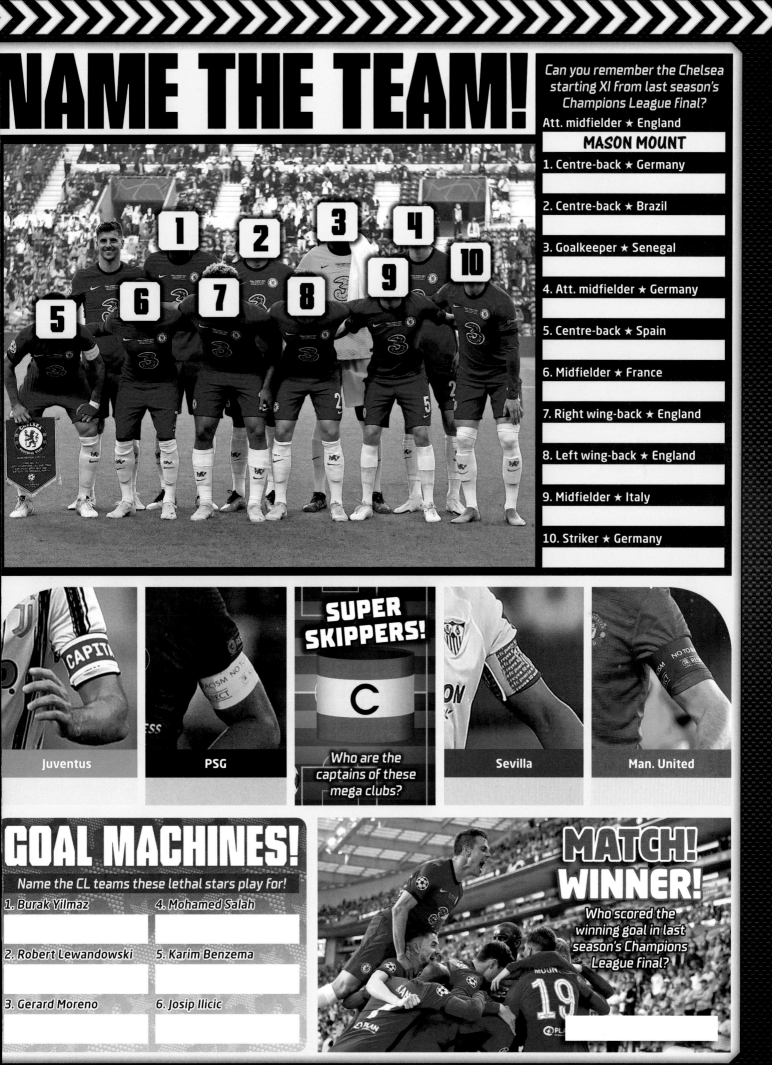

Att. midfielder ★ England
MASON MOUNT

1. Centre-back ★ Germany

2. Centre-back ★ Brazil

3. Goalkeeper ★ Senegal

4. Att. midfielder ★ Germany

5. Centre-back ★ Spain

6. Midfielder ★ France

7. Right wing-back ★ England

8. Left wing-back ★ England

9. Midfielder ★ Italy

10. Striker ★ Germany

SUPER SKIPPERS!

Who are the captains of these mega clubs?

Juventus

PSG

Sevilla

Man. United

GOAL MACHINES!

Name the CL teams these lethal stars play for!

1. Burak Yilmaz

2. Robert Lewandowski

3. Gerard Moreno

4. Mohamed Salah

5. Karim Benzema

6. Josip Ilicic

MATCH! WINNER!

Who scored the winning goal in last season's Champions League final?

ANSWERS ON PAGE 94

Champions League BRAIN-BUSTER!

How well do you know Europe's biggest club comp?

1. True or False? Only two teams have progressed past the group stage without winning any of their first five games!

2. Which legendary Champions League-winning midfielder is older – Xavi or Andres Iniesta?

3. Which Portuguese club did Spanish champions Atletico Madrid sign Joao Felix from in the summer of 2019?

4. When did Italian giants Juventus last reach the Champions League final?

5. Which club did new Man. United winger Jadon Sancho play for in the Champions League last season?

6. Who became the youngest-ever top goalscorer in the history of the competition in 2020-21?

7. Before leaving last summer, how many times did Sergio Ramos win the Champions League with Real Madrid?

8. What African country did legendary Champions League goal grabber Samuel Eto'o play for?

9. Which manager has won the most CLs – Thomas Tuchel, Pep Guardiola, Carlo Ancelotti or Diego Simeone?

10. Which country has AC Milan's Zlatan Ibrahimovic not played in – Sweden, Italy, United States or Germany?

1 ....
2 ....
3 ....
4 ....
5 ....
6 ....
7 ....
8 ....
9 ....
10 ....

ANSWERS ON PAGE 94

BUILD YOUR OWN CLUB!

Ever wanted to create your own epic footy club? Well now you can! Design your kit, select your stadium, pick your team and loads more. GO!

Write your team name here:

....

DESIGN YOUR KIT!

First things first, and one of the most important things to decide – how are your team going to look? Think about what colours you want to send them out in and what style kit you want! Will you go for something simple and classy, or a mashed-up crazy design? We've picked out some eye-catching kits below to give you some inspiration...

EPIC NEW 2021-22 KITS!

Newcastle

Arsenal

Watford

Crystal Palace

CRAZY KITS!

Bordeaux
Third 2016-17

Mexico
Home 1998

Norwich
Third 2016-17

England
Goalkeeper 1996

Man. City
Third 2020-21

CLASSIC KITS!

Peru
Home 2019

Barcelona
Home 2012-13

England
Home 1980-83

Brazil
Home 1998

Denmark
Away 1992

DRAW YOUR BADGE!

Your club crest tells fans who you are and what you stand for! Check out some famous badges, then see if you can come up with something that'll be recognised all over the world!

CREATE YOUR MASCOT!

How will you choose one of the main faces of your club – base it on your team's nickname, the design of your badge, or something totally random? Take a look at some of the top clubs' mascots for ideas...

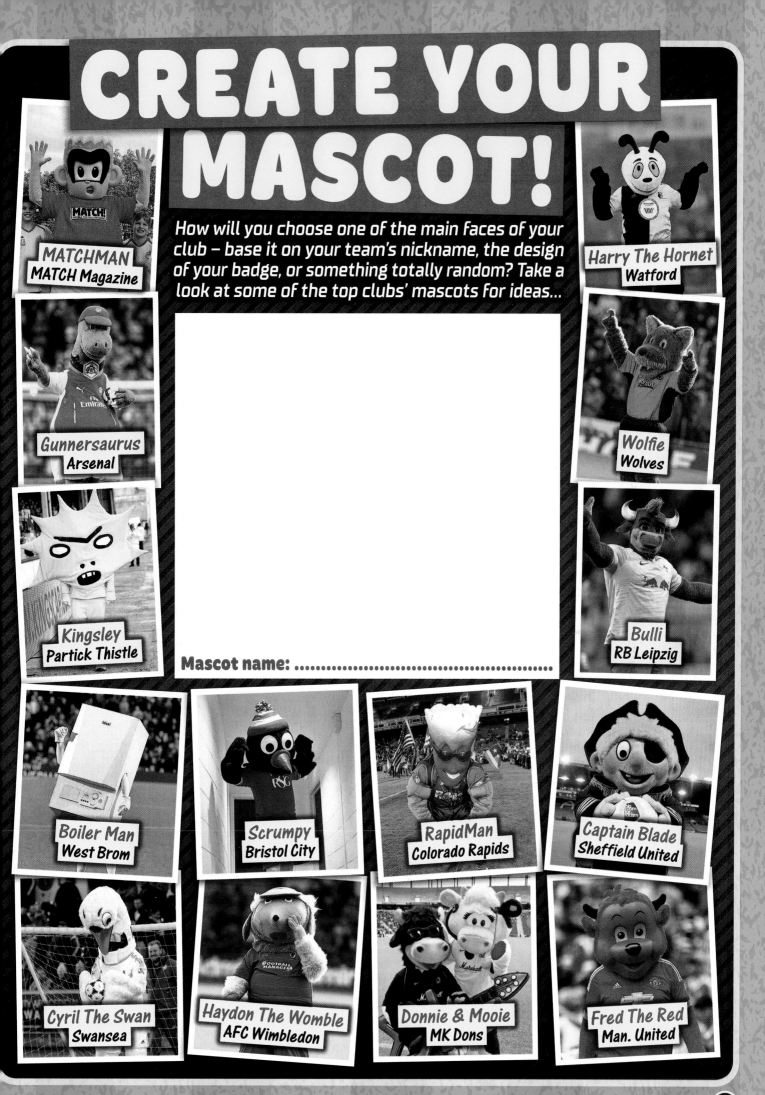

MATCHMAN
MATCH Magazine

Harry The Hornet
Watford

Gunnersaurus
Arsenal

Wolfie
Wolves

Kingsley
Partick Thistle

Bulli
RB Leipzig

Mascot name: ....

Boiler Man
West Brom

Scrumpy
Bristol City

RapidMan
Colorado Rapids

Captain Blade
Sheffield United

Cyril The Swan
Swansea

Haydon The Womble
AFC Wimbledon

Donnie & Mooie
MK Dons

Fred The Red
Man. United

PICK YOUR FACILITIES!

Now it's time to decide where you want your team to play! You'll also need to pick your training ground, academy and footballs, but you can only pick one gold, two silvers and one bronze, so choose wisely!

GOLD STADIUMS

Nou Camp
Capacity: **99,354**

Wembley Stadium
Capacity: **90,000**

Signal Iduna Park
Capacity: **81,365**

Bernabeu
Capacity: **81,044**

Ataturk Olympic Stadium
Capacity: **74,753**

Stade Velodrome
Capacity: **67,394**

Puskas Arena
Capacity: **67,215**

Estadio da Luz
Capacity: **64,642**

Tottenham Hotspur Stadium
Capacity: **62,850**

SILVER STADIUMS

Red Bull Arena
Capacity: **42,959**

Villa Park
Capacity: **42,095**

Ramon Sanchez Pizjuan
Capacity: **43,883**

Vodafone Park
Capacity: **42,590**

Juventus Stadium
Capacity: **41,507**

St. Jakob-Park
Capacity: **38,512**

Parken Stadium
Capacity: **38,065**

Philips Stadion
Capacity: **35,000**

Partizan Stadium
Capacity: **29,775**

BRONZE STADIUMS

Ashton Gate
Capacity: **27,000**

The Hawthorns
Capacity: **26,688**

Pittodrie
Capacity: **20,866**

Liberty Stadium
Capacity: **21,088**

Selhurst Park
Capacity: **25,486**

Easter Road
Capacity: **20,421**

Craven Cottage
Capacity: **25,700**

Turf Moor
Capacity: **21,994**

Tynecastle
Capacity: **20,099**

My pick:

GOLD TRAINING GROUNDS

England St. George's Park

Bayern Munich Sabener Strasse

Man. City Etihad Campus

SILVER TRAINING GROUNDS

Leicester Seagrave

Lille Domaine de Luchin

Celtic Lennoxtown

BRONZE TRAINING GROUNDS

Everton Finch Farm

Hertha Berlin Schenkendorfplatz

Newcastle Darsley Park

My pick:

GOLD FOOTBALL

Champions League ball

SILVER FOOTBALL

Premier League ball

BRONZE FOOTBALL

EFL ball

My pick:

GOLD ACADEMY

You've got tons of young talent! Loads of your squad came through the academy, while others get sold for big bucks!

SILVER ACADEMY

Every now and then a real star breaks through into the first team, but you have to loan most out to help them improve!

BRONZE ACADEMY

The players that come through your academy look ultra promising, but often fail to make it to the first team!

My pick:

PICK YOUR TEAM!

Now for the most important part – pick your squad! Check out all of these players, before deciding who you want for your final XI. You can pick no more than four golds, four silvers and four bronzes – and any player you want who's not listed here counts as a bronze!

GOLD PLAYERS

Thibaut Courtois
Real Madrid – GK

Virgil van Dijk
Liverpool – CB

Kevin De Bruyne
Man. City – CM/AM

Neymar
PSG – WG/ST

Gianluigi Donnarumma PSG – GK	**Marquinhos** PSG – CB	**N'Golo Kante** Chelsea – CM	**Kylian Mbappe** PSG – WG/ST
Jan Oblak Atletico Madrid – GK	**Ruben Dias** Man. City – CB	**Luka Modric** Real Madrid – CM	**Erling Haaland** Borussia Dortmund – ST
Trent Alexander-Arnold Liverpool – RB	**Raphael Varane** Man. United – CB	**Mohamed Salah** Liverpool – WG	**Cristiano Ronaldo** Man. United – ST
Joshua Kimmich Bayern Munich – RB/CM	**Andy Robertson** Liverpool – LB	**Lionel Messi** PSG – WG/ST	**Robert Lewandowski** Bayern Munich – ST

Joao Cancelo
Man. City – RB/LB

Alphonso Davies
Bayern Munich – LB

Bruno Fernandes
Man. United – CM/AM

Harry Kane
Tottenham – ST

SILVER PLAYERS

Edouard Mendy
Chelsea - GK

Harry Maguire
Man. United - CB

Frenkie de Jong
Barcelona - CM

Raheem Sterling
Man. City - WG

Manuel Neuer Bayern Munich - GK	**John Stones** Man. City - CB	**Declan Rice** West Ham - CM	**Jadon Sancho** Man. United - WG
Emiliano Martinez Aston Villa - GK	**Sergio Ramos** PSG - CB	**Mason Mount** Chelsea - CM/AM	**Marcus Rashford** Man. United - WG/ST
Aaron Wan-Bissaka Man. United - RB	**David Alaba** Real Madrid - CB/LB	**Phil Foden** Man. City - AM/WG	**Ciro Immobile** Lazio - ST
Joakim Maehle Atalanta - RB/LB	**Luke Shaw** Man. United - LB	**Jack Grealish** Man. City - AM/WG	**Romelu Lukaku** Chelsea - ST

Reece James
Chelsea - RB

Leonardo Spinazzola
Roma - LB

Son Heung-min
Tottenham - WG

Karim Benzema
Real Madrid - ST

BRONZE PLAYERS

Yann Sommer
Borussia Monchengladbach - GK

Dayot Upamecano
Bayern Munich - CB

Tomas Soucek
West Ham - CM

Bukayo Saka
Arsenal - LB/WG/AM

Illan Meslier Leeds - GK	**Tyrone Mings** Aston Villa - CB	**Billy Gilmour** Norwich - CM	**Harvey Barnes** Leicester - WG/AM
Jordan Pickford Everton - GK	**Ben White** Arsenal - CB	**Pierre-Emile Hojbjerg** Tottenham - CM	**Danny Ings** Aston Villa - ST
Vladimir Coufal West Ham - RB	**Kieran Tierney** Arsenal - LB	**Youri Tielemans** Leicester - CM	**Patrick Bamford** Leeds - ST
Denzel Dumfries Inter - RB	**Jose Gaya** Valencia - LB	**Emiliano Buendia** Aston Villa - WG/AM	**Gerard Moreno** Villarreal - ST

Ricardo Pereira
Leicester - RB

Ben Davies
Tottenham - LB

Jude Bellingham
B. Dortmund - CM

Dominic Calvert-Lewin
Everton - ST

CHOOSE YOUR MANAGER!

Now pick your gaffer! You should have a gold, silver or bronze left over after picking your players, so use that to select your boss!

GOLD MANAGERS

Jurgen Klopp
Liverpool

Pep Guardiola
Man. City

Mauricio Pochettino
PSG

Diego Simeone
Atletico Madrid

SILVER MANAGERS

Unai Emery
Villarreal

Jose Mourinho
Roma

Brendan Rodgers
Leicester

Julian Nagelsmann
Bayern Munich

BRONZE MANAGERS

Marcelo Bielsa
Leeds

Gian Piero Gasperini
Atalanta

Sean Dyche
Burnley

David Moyes
West Ham

CHOOSE YOUR STYLE!

FORMATIONS

You've picked your XI, so now you need to work out how they're going to line up! Select the best formation to suit your players – or go back and change some of your XI if none of the systems work out! Then finally choose your tactics, before turning over to complete your club!

4-4-2

		GK		
RB	CB		CB	LB
WG/AM	CM		CM	WG/AM
	ST		ST	

4-3-3

		GK		
RB	CB		CB	LB
	CM	CM	CM	
	WG/ST	ST	WG/ST	

3-5-2

		GK		
RB/CB		CB		LB/CB
RB/WG	CM	AM/CM	CM	LB/WG
	ST		ST	

4-2-3-1

		GK		
RB	CB		CB	LB
	CM		CM	
WG/AM		AM		WG/AM
		ST		

3-4-3

		GK		
RB/CB		CB		LB/CB
RB/WG	CM		CM	LB/WG
	WG/ST	ST	WG/ST	

TACTICS

Counter-attack
Leicester

Possession
Man. City

Long ball
Burnley

High press
Liverpool

MY TEAM!

Add your team below and in formation on the pitch, then email photos to:
match.magazine@kelsey.co.uk

My Players:

My Manager:

My Tactics:

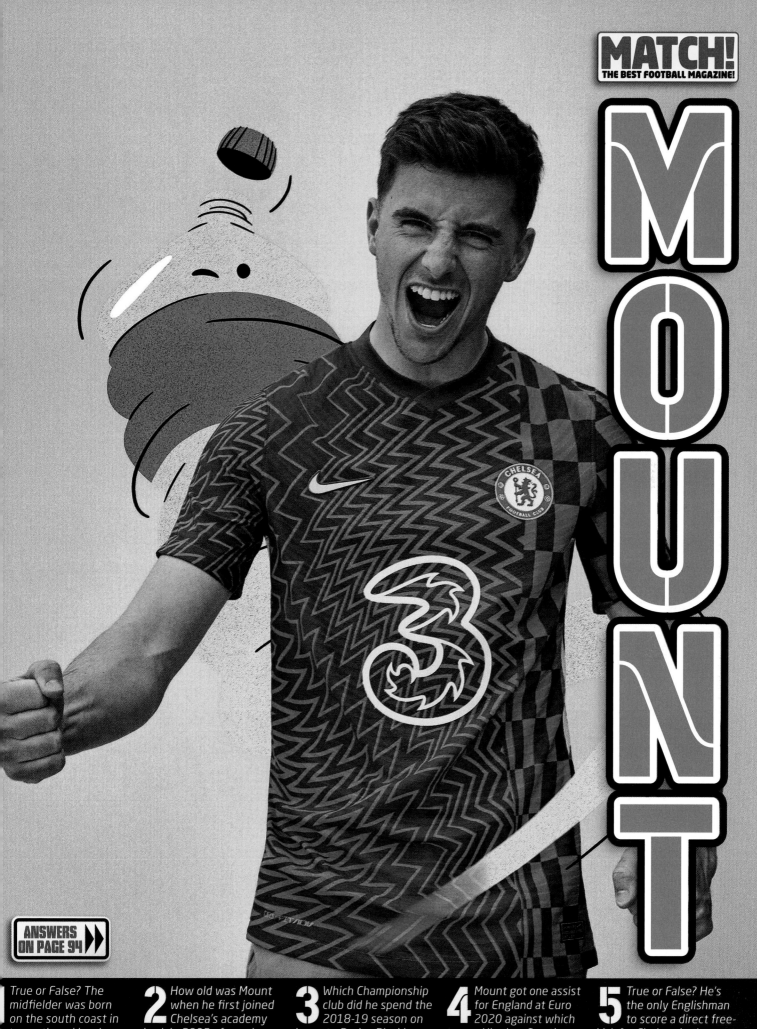

MATCH!
THE BEST FOOTBALL MAGAZINE!

MOUNT

ANSWERS ON PAGE 94 ▶▶

1 True or False? The midfielder was born on the south coast in Portsmouth and has been a lifelong Pompey fan!

2 How old was Mount when he first joined Chelsea's academy back in 2005 - four, six or eight years old?

3 Which Championship club did he spend the 2018-19 season on loan at - Derby, Blackburn or Nottingham Forest?

4 Mount got one assist for England at Euro 2020 against which team - Ukraine, Croatia, Denmark or Italy?

5 True or False? He's the only Englishman to score a direct free-kick for Chelsea in the Premier League!

2022'S A BIG YEAR FOR...
ALEXANDER-ARNOLD

THE STORY SO FAR...

The Liverpool lad has a point to prove in 2022!

Trent made his debut for his boyhood club in 2016, quickly establishing himself as first-choice right-back and one of Europe's top young talents! He scored his first goal v Hoffenheim in the Champions League, and was a key man on the road to the 2018 final!

After that, Trent went from strength to strength. Under Jurgen Klopp, he's become more than just a right-back - he's also the team's main creator! He racked up tons of assists as Liverpool won the CL in 2019, and then lifted the Prem title a year later!

2020-21 was the first disappointment of Trent's career. He struggled to hit the heights of the year before as Liverpool failed to defend their league title, then he picked up an injury in England's final warm-up game before the Euros to miss the tournament!

REDS BACK ON TOP?

In his short career, Alexander-Arnold has quickly got used to competing for major trophies, so last season's third-place finish and Champions League quarter-final exit will have stung. If Liverpool are going to get back to winning silverware, their local lad at right-back will play a massive role - when he's on form, he can create tons of chances for The Reds' awesome attack!

WORLD CUP PUSH!

Even before injury ruled him out of Euro 2020, Trent wasn't a guaranteed starter for England - Kyle Walker, Reece James and Kieran Trippier were often picked ahead of him - so he needs to start taking his club form to the international stage. He only had a limited role at the 2018 World Cup, so the Qatar World Cup will be his first chance to properly showcase his talent at a major tournament!

NEXT KIMMICH?

When he was in Liverpool's academy Trent played in midfield, but switched to right-back to give himself a better shot of making the first team. But now that he's established, we could see him switch around - just like Joshua Kimmich! The Bayern man first burst onto the scene as an attacking full-back, but now he bosses games from centre mid - could Trent do the same?

CAPTAIN FANTASTIC?

Jordan Henderson is the current captain of Liverpool, with James Milner his deputy and Virgil van Dijk next in line after that. But all three of them have had injury woes, so don't be surprised to see Trent wearing the armband at some stage in 2022. He's already captained the side before, and would love to get the job permanently - like his all-time football idol, Steven Gerrard!

2022 IN NUMBERS...

13
Trent would love to beat his own record for PL assists by a defender in a single season!

53
The all-time PL record for assists by a defender is 53, and Trent has that in his sights too!

79
Trent only played 79 minutes at the 2018 World Cup – he'll be desperate to get way more than that in Qatar!

200
He's on track to play his 200th game for Liverpool in 2022 – and he'll be one of the youngest players to hit that milestone!

YOU'LL NEVER WALK ALONE
LIVERPOOL
FOOTBALL CLUB
EST·1892

SNAPPED!
BEST OF 2021!

Camera check!

Nicolas Pepe wanted to make sure the cameraman captured his goal!

YEP, THAT'S ME!

The Dortmund guys were getting snapped for their next album cover!

CAN'T WAIT FOR OUR WORLD TOUR!

Borussia boy band!

THAT'S 180!

Maximum checkout!

So that's what James Maddison gets up to in his spare time

I CAN'T FEEL MY FEET!

Was Hector playing against West Brom or Antarctica?

Bracing Bellerin!

Hand of God!

Olivier Giroud tried his best Diego Maradona impression!

WHAT A HEADER!

BIG MATCH! QUIZ

WSL SPECIAL

crazy names!

Which WSL clubs have these nicknames?

1. The Royals

2. The Gunners

3. The Seagulls

4. The Toffees

5. The Foxes

6. The Red Devils

TRUE or FALSE?

Read these statements and work out if they're true or false!

1. Man. United did the double over arch-rivals Man. City last season!

2. North London giants Tottenham were relegated from the Women's Super League last season!

3. Sam Kerr became the first Australian to win the WSL Golden Boot in 2020-21!

4. There are 18 teams in the WSL!

5. Mega rivals Chelsea and Arsenal have won more WSL titles than the rest of the league put together!

CAMERA SHY!

Can you name the players hiding from the MATCH snapper in the WSL last season?

WSL STARS!

1 **Arsenal** — Arsenal

2 **CHELSEA FOOTBALL CLUB** — Chelsea

3 **MANCHESTER CITY** — Man. City

Match these megastars to the WSL clubs they play for!

Sam Kerr — A

Ellen White — B

Caitlin Foord — C

MYSTERY MASCOT!

Use the clues to work out which Women's Super League club this mascot is from!

↘ My name is Bridget the Lioness and I'm often seen at the Kingsmeadow Stadium!

↘ We've had the same manager since she joined the club in 2012!

↘ I cheer on lethal superstars like Fran Kirby, Bethany England and Pernille Harder. Get in!

SPOT THE BALL!

Mark where you think the ball is in this WSL pic from 2020-21!

THE PRIDE CAZOO CAZOO CAZOO CAZOO

1 2 3 4 5 6 7 8 9 10 11 12 13 14 15 16 17 18 19

2021

2020

GUESS THE WINNERS!
Which team won the Women's Super League in these seasons?

2019

2018

DERBY RIVALS!
Match up the two teams who call each other 'The Enemy!'

1. Arsenal

2. Man. City

3. Aston Villa

A. Birmingham

B. Tottenham

C. Man. United

CRAZY KIT!
Which team wore this mega bright shirt last season?

ANSWERS ON PAGE 94

MEGA WORDSEARCH

Find 40 past and present WSL megastars in the mammoth grid!

Berger	Emslie	Gauvin	Hemp	Ladd	McCabe	Mjelde	Russo
Bronze	England	Graham	Kaagman	Leupolz	Mead	Neville	Toone
Christiansen	Eriksson	Hanson	Kelly	Little	Mewis	Nobbs	Weir
Cuthbert	Foord	Harder	Kerr	Magill	Miedema	Raso	White
Dali	Galton	Harding	Kirby	Mayling	Mitchell	Roord	Williamson

ANSWERS ON PAGE 94

MATCH!
THE BEST FOOTBALL MAGAZINE!

MIEDEMA

ANSWERS ON PAGE 94 ▶▶

1 True or False? The mega lethal Arsenal striker is the all-time leading goalscorer in the Women's Super League!

2 How many goals did Miedema score in her first 100 games for the Netherlands – 53, 63, 73, 83 or 93?

3 Which huge German team did Arsenal sign Vivianne from in 2017 – Bayern Munich, Eintracht Frankfurt or Wolfsburg?

4 She broke the Olympics record in 2021 when she scored how many goals in just four games?

5 True or False? Her younger brother Lars is also a footballer who plays in the second tier of Dutch football!

WORLDY WONDERKID...
LAUREN HEMP!

The epic ENGLAND wonderkid chats about her ambitions with MAN. CITY, her favourite goal and representing her country!

SCORING v ASSISTING!

HEMP SAYS: "You know what, I quite like assisting people! Sometimes I find more joy in that than scoring myself. I like to run with the ball and cross it in, and I like to know that I've done something to help the team. Although I do like to grab a goal now and again!"

BIG AMBITIONS!

HEMP SAYS: "We want to keep going further in the Champions League and hopefully we can win it! Every year the women's game is growing so it's going to keep getting tougher! I really think that with the team we have, it's going to be all up for grabs. We're definitely going to be pushing for every title possible!"

FAVE GOAL!

HEMP SAYS: "I'd probably say it was in my first year at Man. City when I scored in the FA Cup final against West Ham! I came on as a substitute and managed to score at Wembley in front of 40,000 fans! I'd never played in front of a crowd that big, and it was unbelievable! It was a proud moment and to have my family there as well just topped it off!"

RIVALRY WITH MAN. UNITED!

HEMP SAYS: "It's always tough! They've got a good fanbase and it's nice to see. We've got a good fanbase as well, so it's a big rivalry between us and United! It's nice to see them in the WSL so that we've got that derby! You always know that it's going to be a tough game and that it could go either way!"

ENGLAND'S CHANCES!

HEMP SAYS: "I think there's a lot of quality in the squad! When I first arrived at England, it was nice to have a lot of Man. City players there who I've been with every day, and it sort of made that transition a bit easier. There's also a lot of young girls that I played with at the U20 World Cup that are also there. It's a very competitive and talented team!"

EURO 2022!

HEMP SAYS: "I'd love to go to the Euros! It's something that I haven't done yet with the senior team and I'd love to go! A lot of the girls are from Man. City, but there are also players from Chelsea and Arsenal that I get on well with! I'm just hoping to push on and keep improving, and hopefully those call-ups will come!"

PERSONAL TARGETS!

HEMP SAYS: "I've definitely got some goal and assist targets in mind! I don't really want to say what they are as I don't want people to have expectations of me, but I'll definitely push myself! I'll look at where I want to improve and focus on those targets. Hopefully I'll be able to pick up more assists, as well as scoring lots more goals!"

PROUD PARENTS!

HEMP SAYS: "They are such proud parents! We come from a small town in Norfolk, so not a lot comes from there. It's full of farms, so they don't see the big cities! They are really proud of me, and I think they do miss me a bit even though they hate to say it! They always love to get to as many games as they possibly can!"

COMPETING WITH CHELSEA!

HEMP SAYS: "They're very tough! Whenever we play them at home, they're always hard to beat, but I do love those games! They're the sort of games that you want to be involved in. I'm lucky enough to have played in a few since joining Man. City!"

MATCH! CHATS TO WSL STARS!

MATCH chatted to tons of Women's Super League stars in 2020–21! Get a load of the best quotes that featured in our magazine over the past 12 months...

MAYA LE TISSIER

Brighton baller Maya Le Tissier gave MATCH some inside knowledge on her team-mates, including who's the funniest...

MAYA SAYS: "I would probably say Aileen Whelan! She gets bored very easily so is always joking about or, as others would say, annoying them by pulling pranks and scaring people! Fliss Gibbons and Victoria Williams would probably be up there too just for the funny things that they come out with!"

KIRSTY HANSON

The Man. United ace recalls the first-ever live footy match she went to watch as a child!

KIRSTY SAYS: "I can't remember for sure, but I think it might have been Burnley against Arsenal at Turf Moor. I think I was about nine years old at the time. My brother supports Arsenal, so my mum got tickets and I went along with him. I think Arsenal won 2-0. It was very cold, but a great atmosphere!"

MAZ PACHECO

We asked the Aston Villa star for a piece of information people wouldn't already know about her...

MAZ SAYS: "I'm actually a qualified scuba diver! I learnt when I was on holiday in the Philippines. The ocean is unbelievable there, it's like paradise. One of my fondest memories is scuba diving with sharks. I'm certain I saw the real life Nemo and Dory swimming together, so who wouldn't love that!"

HANNAH HAMPTON

We'd love to know what the ex-Birmingham goalkeeper is learning right now!

HANNAH SAYS: "I'm not really a series or film watcher – I can't sit still and concentrate for that long! I always have to be doing something to keep me occupied, and I prefer to learn new skills. My favourite hobby would be playing the piano and guitar - I enjoy being self-taught and I like the challenge of learning new songs!"

ELLA TOONE

We weren't too shocked when we found out who lifelong Man. United fan Ella Toone wanted to play like...

ELLA SAYS: "My hero growing up was Cristiano Ronaldo. When he played for Man. United I used to watch clips on YouTube of him doing his skills in matches, and then I'd go out into the garden and practise them! I loved the way he played, his passion for the game and just how hard-working he is. I wanted to be just like him and just as skilful as him!"

GABBY GEORGE

The Everton legend could've been a sprinter if she hadn't become a footy star!

GABBY SAYS: "I think I would've stuck to athletics and maybe tried to take that path! I used to be ranked No.1 in the north west for 200 metres. I was sports mad as a child and never dreamt of another job, although I did want to be a shop keeper to sit at the till and pass the items through, but I do that on the self service now – so best of both worlds!"

JILL ROORD

There's no surprise Dutch duo Jill Roord and Vivianne Miedema have such a magical connection on the pitch...

JILL SAYS: "I have many friends in football, but my best friend is Vivianne Miedema – we've known each other since we were around 12 years old, and we have always had a special connection both on and off the pitch!"

ROSELLA AYANE

We wanted to know what the Spurs star would be if she wasn't a professional footballer...

ROSELLA SAYS: "If I wasn't a footballer, I'd love to be a doctor of some kind! I'm not sure what I'd specialise in, but when I was little I always told my mum I'd be a brain surgeon. If I didn't play football growing up then who knows!"

AIMEE PALMER

We asked the Bristol City midfielder what food she loves and what she avoids!

AIMEE SAYS: "My favourite food is pizza. I love pizza, but I also pretty much like most food. I also really like apples, and I always have an apple a day, but it has to be a Pink Lady. I can't stand sprouts or broccoli, especially when they've been boiled!"

EURO 2020
Scrapbook!

DRIVING FORWARDS!

Italy kicked off the tournament with a thumping 3-0 victory over Turkey, but the show was stolen by the remote control car that brought the match ball onto the pitch!

FOOTBALL UNITES!

Football was forgotten following Christian Eriksen's collapse during Denmark's opening game with Finland. The entire footy world came together, and thankfully he pulled through thanks to the heroics of the medical team and his Danish team-mates.

DUMFRIES RESCUES THE DUTCH!

The Euros properly sparked into life during the Netherlands' epic showdown with Ukraine. The Ukrainians came from two goals down to level it up at 2-2, but then got done by a Dutch sucker-punch!

BOY FROM BRENT!

Raheem Sterling grew up in the shadow of the huge Wembley arch, so he was the perfect man to score England's first goal of the Euros. It was his first goal at a major tournament, too!

SCHICK'S STUNNER!

The Goal of the Tournament competition was over before most teams had even kicked a ball – Patrik Schick's long-range stunner for Czech Republic against Scotland was just ridiculous!

RONALDO'S RECORDS!

Two goals for Cristiano Ronaldo in Portugal's opening game against Hungary saw him pass Michel Platini as the European Championship's all-time top scorer! He ended with five goals and the Golden Boot!

WALES' BIG GUNS DELIVER!

Wales had to beat Turkey to stand a chance of reaching the last 16 – and that's exactly what they did! Star men Gareth Bale and Aaron Ramsey were on top form!

ENGLAND-SCOTLAND SNORE-FEST!

Scotland's trip to Wembley to face England was a repeat of their epic Euro '96 showdown, but it totally failed to live up to the hype. The 0-0 draw was rubbish!

PANDEV'S GUARD OF HONOUR!

North Macedonia legend Goran Pandev was one of the oldest outfielders to ever play at the Euros, and he was given a proper send-off in his last-ever international game v the Netherlands!

DENMARK BATTER RUSSIA!

Denmark's players were absolute heroes to bounce back from their traumatic first game to seal a place in the last 16. They blew Russia away with a 4-1 win in an electric atmosphere in Copenhagen!

MODRIC MAGIC SENDS OUT SCOTLAND!

Only a win would do for Scotland in their final group game against Croatia, but Luka Modric produced a masterclass with a worldy goal and an assist to end their last-16 hopes!

EURO 2020 Scrapbook!

DUBRAVKA STINKER!

Spain only scored once in their first two matches, but bagged five in their last group game v Slovakia. Goalkeeper Martin Dubravka gave them a hand though, with one of the worst own goals the Euros has ever seen!

HUNGARY GO CLOSE TO HISTORY!

Hungary almost produced one of the Euros' biggest-ever shocks. With six minutes remaining, The Magyars led Germany 2-1, but Leon Goretzka came to the rescue of the three-time European champions!

WALES BLOWN AWAY!

Wales couldn't repeat the magic of Euro 2016 when they made it to the semi-finals. They were smashed in the last 16 4-0 by Denmark, who were beginning to look like serious contenders!

CZECHS STUN NETHERLANDS!

Netherlands were hot favourites to reach the quarter-finals but, after centre-back Matthijs de Ligt was sent off for a crazy handball, Czech Republic claimed a shock 2-0 victory!

MAD MONDAY: PART 1!

Croatia v Spain had more twists and turns than the world's biggest roller coaster! The Croats had to come from 3-1 down to leave the scores level at full-time, but Spain sealed a 5-3 win in extra-time!

MAD MONDAY: PART 2!

Just hours after the crazy Croatia-Spain clash, France and Switzerland produced even more epic drama! Like Croatia, the Swiss came from 3-1 down to draw 3-3, but went on to dump the world champs out on penalties!

ENGLAND FINALLY BEAT GERMANY!

England hadn't beaten Germany in a knockout game since the 1966 World Cup final, but goals from Raheem Sterling and Harry Kane saw them finally end their wait!

TIME'S UP FOR THE GOLDEN GENERATION!

Belgium's super talented squad cruised into the quarter-finals without breaking sweat, but Kevin De Bruyne, Romelu Lukaku and co. just couldn't find a way past Italy!

HERO TO ZERO!

Alvaro Morata came off the bench to bag an equaliser for Spain v Italy in the semi-finals – but then the striker's shootout miss cost his team a spot in the final. Ouch!

DANISH DREAM ENDS!

Denmark's heroic and surprising run was brought to an end by England in the semi-finals. Harry Kane's extra-time strike put England in their first major tournament final since 1966!

FOOTBALL'S COMING TO ROME!

Luke Shaw scored the quickest-ever goal in a Euros final, but Italy slowly got back on top. After equalising through Leonardo Bonucci, they went on to win on penalties, and England's wait goes on!

BIG MATCH! QUIZ

FOOTBALL LEAGUE SPECIAL

jobswap

BACK TO THE FUTURE

Name the EFL goalscoring legend who has gone back in time as a Roman Gladiator!

Calum Chambers Andre Schurrle Tomas Kalas Lucas Piazon

CLUB SHARERS!

★ ★ ★ ★ ★ ★ ★ ★

Which Championship club have these heroes all played for?

Rui Fonte

Moussa Dembele

FLIPPED!

Name the Championship striker who has had his face messed up in this weird pic!

CAMERA SHY!

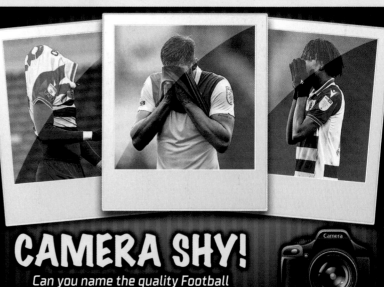

Can you name the quality Football League players hiding in these pics?

5 QUESTIONS ON... NOTTINGHAM FOREST

FOREST

1. Which famous stadium do The Reds play their home matches at?

2. True or False? Forest have been crowned champions of Europe twice!

3. What home nation does rock-solid centre-back Scott McKenna play for?

4. Can you name Forest's big East Midlands rivals in the Championship?

5. How old is their tricky winger Joe Lolley – 26, 27, 28 or 29 years old?

GUESS THE WINNERS!

Which teams won League One in these seasons?

2021

2019

2018

2017

MICK GEORGE GROUP

1.

GREAT ANNUAL SAVINGS GROUP

2.

CHANSIRI

3.

🔍 SPOT THE SPONSOR!

Name the teams who had these sponsors on their shirts last season!

ideal BOILERS

4.

ecotricity

5.

MICK GEORGE GROUP

6.

MATCH! WINNER!

Who scored a brace for Blackpool against Lincoln in last season's League One play-off final?

?

ANSWERS ON PAGE 94

CROSSWORD CRUNCH!

Use these clues to fill in our Football League crossword!

ACROSS

1. Shirt number that Andre Ayew used to wear for Swansea! (3)

4. Prem team that Blackburn signed Adam Armstrong from! (9)

6. League One team that Stoke midfielder Nick Powell started his career at! (5)

9. Shirt number that James Vaughan wore for Tranmere! (4)

12. Championship team that England striker Dominic Calvert-Lewin started his career at! (9,6)

13. Position of Bournemouth and Wales' rock-solid superstar Chris Mepham! (8)

17. Number of league goals striker Lucas Joao scored for Reading in 2020-21! (8)

18. National team that David Brooks plays for! (5)

19. League One team that Tom Hopper scores goals for! (7)

20. Country that super-solid Barnsley defender Michal Helik represents! (6)

DOWN

2. Boot brand that attacker Junior Stanislas wears! (4)

3. Nationality of West Brom gaffer Valerien Ismael! (6)

5. League One team that Leicester's goalscoring hero Jamie Vardy supports! (9,9)

7. Month that Cardiff hero Kieffer Moore was born! (6)

8. League Two club that ex-Rochdale goal king Ian Henderson now plays for! (7)

10. East Midlands side that Kamil Jozwiak plays for! (5)

11. Premier League team that Reading signed midfielder Ovie Ejaria from in 2020! (9)

14. League One team that Swansea signed Jamaica goal king Jamal Lowe from! (5)

15. Foot that QPR target man Lyndon Dykes prefers to use! (5)

16. Cool country that Ben Brereton represented at the 2021 Copa America! (5)

ANSWERS ON PAGE 94

MATCH!
THE BEST FOOTBALL MAGAZINE!

IBRAHIMOVIC

ANSWERS ON PAGE 94 ▶▶

1 Which Swedish city was Ibrahimovic born in back in 1981 Orebro, Gothenburg, tockholm or Malmo?

2 Which French team did he score twice against on his Champions League debut for Ajax in 2002 - Lille, PSG or Lyon?

3 How many league goals did Zlatan score in his one and only season for Barcelona - more or less than 20?

4 Which other sport was Zlatan really good at growing up - judo, taekwondo, ice hockey or tennis?

5 Which of these teams has he never played for - AC Milan, Inter, LA Galaxy, PSG, Juventus, Man. United or Real Madrid!

FIFA FLOPS!
WONDERKIDS EDITION!

Who doesn't love signing a wonderkid on FIFA? Unfortunately, it doesn't always work out as planned! MATCH has been checking out some former prospects who haven't lived up to their in-game potential!

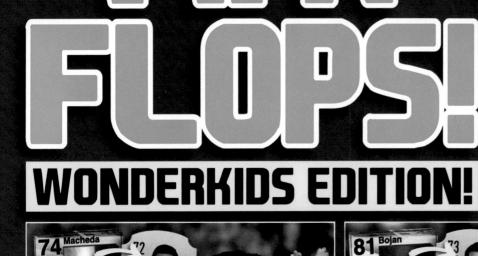

74 Macheda
ST

MACHEDA
69 PAC	70 DRI
73 SHO	30 DEF
58 PAS	62 PHY

72

75 PAC	72 DRI
74 SHO	50 DEF
50 PAS	71 HEA

FEDERICO MACHEDA
FIFA 10 POTENTIAL: 88
FIFA 21 RATING: 72

It's been over 12 years since Macheda scored 'that goal' on his debut for Man. United against Aston Villa as a 17-year-old! He was expected to become a star at Old Trafford, but he has since ended up in Greece with Panathinaikos after a string of disappointing moves in England!

81 Bojan
CF

73

BOJAN
69 PAC	77 DRI
70 SHO	27 DEF
73 PAS	43 PHY

86 PAC	86 DRI
74 SHO	48 DEF
75 PAS	60 HEA

BOJAN
FIFA 10 POTENTIAL: 88
FIFA 21 RATING: 73

Given that he's a distant cousin of megastar Lionel Messi, it's perhaps no surprise that Bojan was so highly-rated when he broke through at Barcelona! He did manage to make over 100 appearances at the Nou Camp, but certainly didn't reach the heights many expected of him!

BAKKALI
73 | RW

BASIC
85 PAC	84 DRI
68 SHO	34 DEF
60 PAS	38 HEA

69

BAKKALI
74 PAC	76 DRI
68 SHO	19 DEF
62 PAS	54 PHY

ZAKARIA BAKKALI
FIFA 14 POTENTIAL: 90
FIFA 21 RATING: 69

The 17-year-old wing wizard was one of the best wonderkids on FIFA 14! If you managed him correctly, the Belgian had the potential to develop into a 90-rated star! Unfortunately, it hasn't worked out for him since, and he was given a really disappointing card on FIFA 21!

69 Butland
GK 4-1-2-1-...

74

BUTLAND
74 DIV	76 REF
68 HAN	57 SPD
66 KIC	76 POS

70 DIV	75 REF
67 HAN	67 SPD
55 KIC	66 POS

JACK BUTLAND
FIFA 13 POTENTIAL: 85
FIFA 21 RATING: 74

Butland definitely isn't the only Englishman to have been overhyped as a youngster! He was seen as England's future No.1 when he first broke through at Birmingham and Stoke! Even though he returned to the Prem in 2020, he's barely played a game for Crystal Palace!

1 Jack BUTLAN
GOAL 10'

RIECHEDLY BAZOER

FIFA 16 POTENTIAL: 88

FIFA 21 RATING: 72

On FIFA 16, Bazoer was an exciting midfielder with bags of potential! He was an all-rounder with tons of solid ratings for key attributes like tackling, ball control and shooting! He's still a decent player, but just not as good as many thought he might turn out to be a few years ago!

BAZOER 76 CM
76 PAC 79 DRI
63 SHO 67 DEF
75 PAS 75 PHY
BASIC

BAZOER 72
72 PAC 75 DRI
68 SHO 56 DEF
73 PAS 72 PHY

10 Riechedl

GOAL

MAX MEYER

FIFA 15 POTENTIAL: 87

FIFA 21 RATING: 76

Even though he hasn't declined too badly over the last six years on FIFA, midfielder Meyer was expected to be one of Germany's best players by this point in real life! He was tipped to have a long and successful career but recently struggled to even get a game at Crystal Palace!

MEYER 77 CM
BASIC
77 PAC 85 DRI
70 SHO 32 DEF
74 PAS 50 PHY

MEYER 76
67 PAC 80 DRI
62 SHO 64 DEF
77 PAS 64 PHY

REWE

13

VIKTOR FISCHER

FIFA 14 POTENTIAL: 86

FIFA 21 RATING: 74

As a 19-year-old Ajax winger on FIFA 14, Fischer already had more than enough about him to cause defenders all sorts of problems! Now at Copenhagen, he's gone from having the potential to become an 86-rated player on FIFA 14, to just a 74 OVR on FIFA 21. Ouch!

FISCHER 74 LW
BASIC
78 PAC 82 DRI
71 SHO 46 DEF
66 PAS 50 HEA

FISCHER 74
82 PAC 75 DRI
70 SHO 35 DEF
70 PAS 68 PHY

7 Viktor FISCHER

GOAL 5'

LUCAS PIAZON

FIFA 14 POTENTIAL: 85

FIFA 21 RATING: 71

Once tipped for greatness during his time at Chelsea, he's one of many players to fall victim to the loan system at Stamford Bridge – he played just one league game in nine years for The Blues! He was once compared to Brazilian legend Kaka, but he was given just a 71-rated card on FIFA 21!

PIAZON 77 LW
BASIC
76 PAC 84 DRI
70 SHO 43 DEF
74 PAS 59 HEA

LUCAS PIAZON 71
65 PAC 73 DRI
71 SHO 34 DEF
72 PAS 51 PHY

MICHY BATSHUAYI

FIFA 14 POTENTIAL: 86

FIFA 21 RATING: 78

Belgium super sub Batshuayi looked as though he could develop into a sick striker, but it hasn't worked out for him at all at Chelsea – he's been loaned out loads and the goals have dried up big time! He's still got an elite goalscoring record at international level, though!

BATSHUAYI 73 ST
BASIC
80 PAC 75 DRI
74 SHO 47 DEF
56 PAS 70 HEA

BATSHUAYI 78
75 PAC 78 DRI
79 SHO 33 DEF
58 PAS 72 PHY

23 Michy BATSHUAYI

GOAL 2'

W88

JOSH MCEACHRAN

FIFA 12 POTENTIAL: 83

FIFA 21 RATING: 68

McEachran also started his career at Chelsea, but it's safe to say he's seen a much bigger drop off than the likes of Piazon and Batshuayi! He's had to drop all the way down to League One in search of regular first-team football and is currently playing for Milton Keynes Dons. Crazy!

McEachran 71 CM
4-2
76 PAC 75 DRI
64 SHO 58 DEF
74 PAS 50 HEA

MCEACHRAN 68
61 PAC 71 DRI
46 SHO 63 DEF
71 PAS 52 PHY

SUZUKI

2022'S A BIG YEAR FOR...
MESSI

Can the Argentina magician take PSG to the next level?

THE STORY SO FAR...

Everybody knows Leo's story! He left Argentina to join Barcelona's La Masia academy when he was just a child, and went on to become their greatest-ever player, smashing the all-time goal record and winning every trophy in sight!

But, after Barca won the treble in 2015, things have slowly gone downhill. They've only reached the Champions League semi-finals once since then – when they threw away a 3-0 lead against Liverpool – and in 2020 Messi handed in a transfer request!

Barcelona eventually convinced him to stay, and he was ready to retire at the club – but that didn't go to plan! With absolutely massive debts, the club simply couldn't afford to keep him, and Messi walked away from the club he loves to join PSG...

MNM THE NEW MSN?

Messi has played in some incredible front threes during his goal-packed career, starring alongside legends like Ronaldinho, Samuel Eto'o, Thierry Henry, Luis Suarez and Neymar. But now that he's been reunited with the Brazilian trickster, plus France megastar Kylian Mbappe, he might be in the deadliest trio ever now! To prove it, they need goals and trophies galore!

TITLE WINNERS?

Last season was a total disaster for PSG, as they missed out on the French title for the first time since 2017 - getting pipped on the last day by surprise winners Lille! Their first priority has to be getting back on top in Ligue 1, and Messi will play a big part in that – he's scored at least 25 league goals in each of the last 12 seasons, and he should easily continue that record in France!

THE HOLY GRAIL!

Winning the Champions League has been PSG's top target ever since they were taken over back in 2011. But now they've signed Messi - plus fellow new boys Sergio Ramos, Achraf Hakimi, Georginio Wijnaldum and Euro 2020 Player of the Tournament Gianluigi Donnarumma - it's not just a target, it's an absolute must! There's huge pressure on Leo - can he deliver?

WORLD CUP GLORY?

Winning a major international trophy has hung over Messi's head for ages - until last summer when he finally fired Argentina to Copa America glory in arch-rivals Brazil's own back yard! He'd love to back that up by winning the World Cup in Qatar and, if he pulls it off, he'll have to move clear of footy legend Diego Maradona as his country's greatest-ever player!

2022 IN NUMBERS...

5
Messi is chasing his fifth Champions League trophy – only one player has won more than that in football history!

3
If he can win Ligue 1, the French Cup and the Champo League, he'll become the first player to win three trebles!

7
Messi's already won a record six European Golden Shoe awards, and is chasing his seventh!

2
Messi only needs to play twice in Qatar to match Maradona's World Cup appearance record for Argentina!

WIN!

EPOS H3 HEADSET!

Take your gaming to the next level with the awesome EPOS H3 Headset! The closed acoustic headset delivers an immersive experience with multi-platform plug and play use – and we've got eight to give away!

For more info on this elite headset and tons of other jaw-dropping gear, visit www.eposaudio.com

EPOS

The lightweight, adjustable headband also features hinged ear cups that angle to fit any face shape!

The EPOS H3 headset delivers skin-tingling audio and extreme comfort for long gaming sessions, plus comes in black or white colourways!

CLOSING DATE: JAN. 31 2022

8 PRIZES!

NACON CONTROLLERS!

The Pro Compact Controller for Xbox boasts a range of customisable features like button mapping, adjustable sticks, trigger sensitivity and vibration motors!

CLOSING DATE: JAN. 31 2022

The Camo Revolution Pro Controller 3 is a wicked wired controller for PS, with larger action buttons and triggers, two cool weight compartments and asymmetric sticks!

8 PRIZES!

Thanks to our mates at Nacon, we've got eight controllers to give away – four Pro Compact Controllers for Xbox and four Camo Revolution Pro Controller 3 for PlayStation. Get entering right now!

For more info on these incredible controllers and lots of other cool gaming accessories, head over to naconogaming.com and follow @Nacon

nacon

REVOLUTION PRO CONTROLLER 3

HOW TO ENTER! ➤ **WWW.MATCHFOOTBALL.CO.UK**

Then click 'Win' in the navigation bar on the MATCH website. Full T&Cs are available online.

VAN DIJK

ANSWERS ON PAGE 94 ▶▶

Van Dijk scored on his Liverpool debut in January 2018 against which team - Everton, Brighton or Swansea?

2 Which trophy has the powerful Dutchman never won - the Premier League, FA Cup or Champions League?

3 Before joining The Reds, Virgil played for Groningen, Southampton and which massive Scottish side?

4 True or False? He made his debut for Netherlands back in 2015 and is now Oranje's captain!

5 In 2019, he became the first defender to win the PFA Player of the Year award for 14 years - which CB won it in 2005?

The Premier League at 30

In 2022, the Premier League celebrates its 30th birthday, so MATCH has dived into the history books to pick out 30 heroes, villains, winners and losers that have starred over the last three decades...

The Best Team

MAN. CITY, 2017-18

The records that Pep Guardiola's City smashed in 2017-18 were incredible! Not only were they the first and only team to reach 100 points in one season, they finished 19 points ahead of second place, won 32 games and scored 106 goals! Nobody's ever bettered any of those numbers, and maybe never will!

The Worst Team

DERBY COUNTY, 2007-08

Sorry, Rams fans - your club has the tragic title of the worst team the Prem's ever seen! They ended up with just 11 points, only winning one game all season. What a nightmare!

Free-Kick King

DAVID BECKHAM

Becks was the absolute master of whipping balls with curl around helpless walls. He left Man. United almost 20 years ago, but nobody's got anywhere near his record tally of 18 free-kick goals!

Golden Boot

ALAN SHEARER

Everybody knows that Shearer is the Prem's all-time top scorer with 260 goals, but he's got tons of other records too! He's the only player to hit 30 goals three years in a row, scored a record five hat-tricks in one campaign, and is one of only five players to bag five goals in a single game. Legend!

The Grandfather

TEDDY SHERINGHAM

Sheringham was still going strong at the age of 40 when he scored for West Ham to become the oldest player to net in the Prem – three years after becoming the oldest hat-trick scorer. Wowzers!

Golden Gloves

PETR CECH

The Prem has seen some great goalkeepers, but Cech has the stats to take the title! Alongside his record 202 clean sheets, he's also won four Golden Gloves - nobody has more!

Ever-Present

GARETH BARRY

Playing for Aston Villa, Man. City, Everton and West Brom, Barry racked up a record-breaking 653 appearances! Between the 2002-03 and 2012-13 seasons he only missed 35 games!

The Boy Wonder

HARVEY ELLIOTT

Elliott became the Prem's youngest-ever player when he came on for Fulham just a month after turning 16! Shout out to James Vaughan too, the youngest-ever scorer after netting for Everton aged 16 back in 2005!

Greatest Escape

LEICESTER, 2014-15

With nine games of the 2014-15 season left, The Foxes were rooted to the bottom of the table, but then they went and won eight of those games to produce one of the best escapes ever! To make it even better, the following season they won the title!

Mr. Worldwide

CRISTIANO RONALDO

Before he became a legend at Real Madrid and Juventus, CR7 made his name at Man. United. He's the only player ever to win both the Ballon d'Or and European Golden Shoe while playing in the Prem, so he might be the greatest talent the league has ever seen!

Biggest Losers

WEST HAM

Life as a West Ham supporter can be tough at times. In their first 25 Premier League seasons, they lost 394 games - more than any other team in history!

Demon Defence

CHELSEA, 2004-05

Jose Mourinho took the Prem by storm when he took charge of Chelsea in 2004, and they absolutely bossed the league! The most impressive part was that they only conceded 15 goals - a record that still stands!

Goal Machine

MO SALAH, 2017-18

Salah's start to life at Liverpool was nothing short of sensational! Since the Prem went down to 20 teams, nobody's ever scored as many goals as he did in his first year at Anfield when he banged in 32. Legend!

Mr. Mean

PATRICK VIEIRA

The legendary Arsenal captain is one of three players to get eight red cards, but he also got booked a further 76 times! Vieira always tried to dominate the midfield, and often that meant intimidating opponents before they even stepped out onto the pitch!

The Invincibles

ARSENAL

To give you an idea of how hard it is to go through a whole season without losing, the last team to do it before Arsenal were Preston in 1889 when there were still only 12 teams in the league! The Gunners' invincible season of 2003-04 has gone down in history for a good reason!

Disaster Zone

RICHARD DUNNE

With 80 Republic of Ireland caps and over 400 Prem games for Everton, QPR, Man. City and Aston Villa, Dunne was a top-class defender – he just had a terrible habit of putting the ball into his own net! His tally of ten is an all-time PL record!

All-Round Attacker #1

THIERRY HENRY

Some players are great goalscorers, others are quality creators, but it takes a really special player to do both. In 2002-03, Thierry Henry became the first, and only, player to bag 20 goals and 20 assists in one season! The Arsenal legend was totally unstoppable!

All-Round Attacker #2

WAYNE ROONEY

Wazza holds a unique record in Prem history, because he's the only player to have passed both 200 goals and 100 assists! In total he scored or assisted 311 goals – what a legend!

Deadly Duo

FRANK LAMPARD & DIDIER DROGBA

Lampard set up Drogba for 24 of his Prem goals, with the striker returning the favour another 12 times, making the pair the most lethal combo in PL history! The Ivorian bossed opposition centre-backs, while Lamps was a master at arriving late into the box from midfield!

MVPs

HALL OF FAMERS

The Prem introduced their official Hall of Fame in 2021, with Thierry Henry and Alan Shearer the first inductees! They were later joined by Eric Cantona, Roy Keane, Frank Lampard, Dennis Bergkamp, Steven Gerrard and David Beckham!

Assist Machine

KEVIN DE BRUYNE

In 2019-20, the Belgium playmaker matched Thierry Henry's record of 20 assists in one season, and was also the quickest player in PL history to set up 50 goals! He began the 2021-22 campaign in tenth on the all-time list, but has the best ratio of anyone else in the top ten and will definitely bag more!

The Supersub

OLE GUNNAR SOLSKJAER

At the start of the 2021-22 season, nobody had made more appearances as a sub (164) than Liverpool's James Milner, but we have to give this honour to Solskjaer. He once scored four times for Man. United after coming off the bench – against Nottingham Forest in February 1999!

Captain Fantastic

HOME OF THE CHAMPIONS

JOHN TERRY

There's a reason that Chelsea supporters have a banner for their old skipper that says, "Captain, Leader, Legend" – no other Prem captain has guided their team to five titles! Man. United's Roy Keane and City's Vincent Kompany are next on the list with four each!

Mr. Consistent

Goals Galore

EVERTON

The Toffees are one of only six teams to have played in every single Premier League season, but that's brought its own problems! They've conceded over 1,400 goals – more than anyone else! They also have the record for the most draws, with over 300!

STEVEN GERRARD

Players always say that the best honour they can get is recognition from their fellow professionals, so Stevie G must have been phenomenal! He was voted into the PFA Team of the Year a record eight times during the Premier League era!

Silver Medallists

LIVERPOOL

Before they finally got their hands on the Prem title in 2019-20, Liverpool had the record of finishing as runners-up four times without winning the trophy, including the 2018-19 season when they won 97 points - nobody's ever bagged so many without finishing top!

Pure Poacher

ANDY COLE

The ex-Newcastle, Man. United and Blackburn striker is third on the Prem's all-time goal list, but if you take away penalties he goes straight to the top! He also struck 34 goals in one season - a PL record that he shares with Shearer!

Fab Foreigner

SERGIO AGUERO

Only three players are ahead of Aguero on the all-time Prem scorers list - Shearer, Rooney and Andy Cole - making him the most prolific foreign player ever! He's also scored the most goals for a single club (184) and struck a record 12 hat-tricks!

Kings Of The Prem

MAN. UNITED

With a record 13 league titles, there's no doubt that Man. United are the all-time kings of the Premier League! On top of all those trophies, they're also the only team to have scored over 2,000 goals, and will register their 700th victory during the 2021-22 season!

The Boss

SIR ALEX FERGUSON

Man. United would never have won all of those league titles without their legendary gaffer. He was in charge for all 13 of them, and is still miles ahead of Jose Mourinho, Arsene Wenger and Pep Guardiola on the title leader board for managers!

THE BEST ATMOSPHERES IN THE WORLD!

MATCH goes globetrotting to find the stadiums with the best atmospheres in world football!

LA BOMBONERA
Club: Boca Juniors
Country: Argentina
CAPACITY: 54,000

The famous blue and gold of Boca Juniors play their home games in Buenos Aires at La Bombonera! Footy legend, and former Boca hero, Diego Maradona had his own box at the 54,000-capacity stadium which is known for its electric atmosphere - especially in Superclasicos against rivals River Plate! Boca have such a dedicated fanbase that 50,000 supporters once turned up to one of their training sessions. Crazy!

EL MONUMENTAL
Club: River Plate
Country: Argentina
CAPACITY: 70,074

Speaking of River Plate, the Argentine Primera Division giants play at the 70,000-capacity Estadio Antonio Vespucio Liberti, or 'El Monumental', the biggest stadium in Argentina! River have an equally passionate fanbase who regularly contribute to spine-tingling atmospheres at their iconic stadium! As long as you don't support Boca Juniors, it's an amazing experience for any football fan!

RAJKO MITIC STADIUM

Club: Red Star Belgrade
Country: Serbia
CAPACITY: 53,000

Red Star have won the Serbian SuperLiga title for the past four years in a row, and the Rajko Mitic Stadium has helped them achieve that because it's got one of the best atmospheres in world football! They've got a strong base of at least 20,000 hardcore supporters that never stop singing throughout the entirety of every match! If they're playing bitter rivals Partizan Belgrade, then the atmosphere goes up another notch!

ANFIELD

Club: Liverpool
Country: England
CAPACITY: 53,394

Liverpool's stunning fightback against Barcelona in the 2018-19 Champions League was evidence of how much of a difference the atmosphere can make at Anfield! Roared on relentlessly by their fans, The Reds managed to overturn a three-goal deficit from the first leg at the Nou Camp. There's no doubt that Jurgen Klopp's players missed their loyal home support last season!

SIGNAL IDUNA PARK

Club: Borussia Dortmund
Country: Germany
CAPACITY: 81,365

There's no doubt that Dortmund's Signal Iduna Park takes the crown for having the best atmosphere in Germany! The Yellow Wall holds around 25,000 supporters alone and helps create one of the most intimidating atmospheres in Europe! It's so loud that ex-Bayern Munich hero Bastian Schweinsteiger once said that the one thing he feared most from Dortmund was The Yellow Wall!

HONOURABLE MENTIONS

CELTIC PARK
Celtic, Scotland

VODAFONE PARK
Besiktas, Turkey

KARAISKAKIS STADIUM
Olympiakos, Greece

SAN MAMES
Athletic Bilbao, Spain

MARACANA
Flamengo/Fluminense, Brazil

2022'S A BIG YEAR FOR...
SMITH ROWE

THE STORY SO FAR...

Arsenal have great history when it comes to producing young players, and Emile Smith Rowe is just one of the latest top talents to come through their Hale End Academy! Fans have been buzzing about him ever since he was a teenager!

The attacking midfielder's first proper taste of first-team footy came on loan at Huddersfield in the Championship, where he caught the eye with his flair, dribbling ability and creativity. He even scored the goal that kept The Terriers in the league!

Smith Rowe's Arsenal breakthrough came on Boxing Day 2020, when he started against London rivals Chelsea and played a key role in The Gunners' first win in eight Premier League games! Since then he's been a key player in Mikel Arteta's side!

Is Arsenal's new No.10 the man to take them back to the big time?

ARSENAL'S NEW NO.10!

Arteta showed how highly he rates Smith Rowe by handing him the No.10 shirt at the start of the season. That's a big deal at Arsenal - in the past it's been worn by stars like Dennis Bergkamp, Mesut Ozil, Robin van Persie and Jack Wilshere - so the young Gunner has to prove that he's worthy. That means bagging plenty of goals and assists this season!

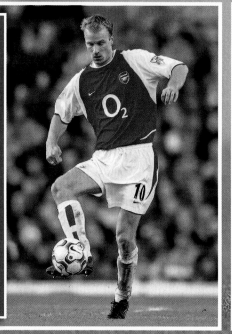

YOUNG GUNNERS!

Smith Rowe isn't the only exciting young star at Arsenal these days - his best mate Bukayo Saka is also set for a massive year for club and country after starring at the Euros for The Three Lions! The pair have the potential to tear it up at The Emirates for years to come, along with the likes of Gabriel Martinelli, Ben White, Albert Sambi Lokonga and Kieran Tierney!

CHAMPIONS LEAGUE CHASE!

The 2017-18 season was the first time in Emile's entire life that Arsenal hadn't been in the Champo League, and they're no closer to getting back there with 2021-22 their first season out of Europe completely since 1996! Returning to Europe's top table is their biggest target, and if ESR can make it happen he'll be an instant club legend!

ENGLAND CALL-UP?

Smith Rowe faces huge competition for places in the England squad with the likes of Mason Mount, Phil Foden, Jack Grealish, Jadon Sancho, Harvey Barnes, Jesse Lingard, James Maddison and Bukayo Saka all vying for attacking midfield spots! It'll be a huge achievement for him to even win his first cap in 2022, but the Under-21 ace will be dreaming of a seat on the plane to Qatar!

2022 IN NUMBERS...

10
Nobody's bagged ten PL assists for The Gunners since 2016-17, so that has to be ESR's top target!

50
If he plays 28 league games this season, he'll reach the epic milestone of 50 Prem appearances – he should clinch it in 2022!

4
Smith Rowe's best goal tally for a single season was four in 2020-21 – he should absolutely smash that record this season!

11
He could become the first Gunner to win the PFA Young Player of the Year since Jack Wilshere in 2011!

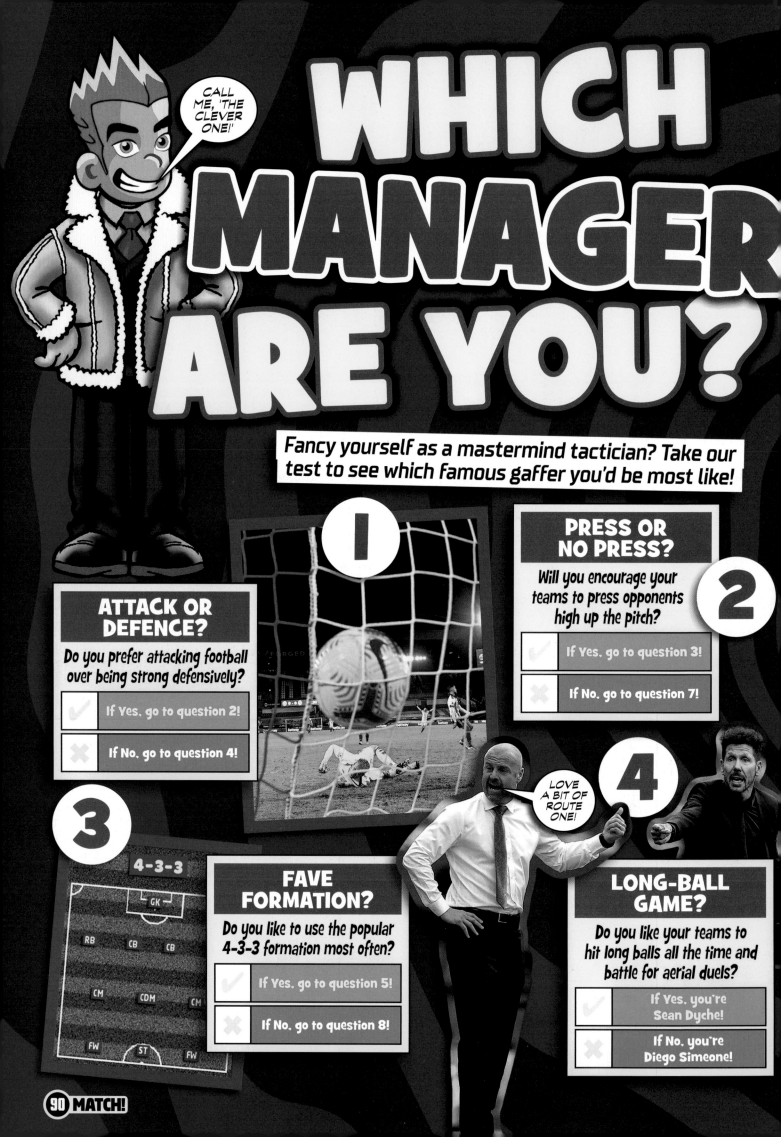

I'M STILL 'THE SPECIAL ONE'!

I'M A FASHION GURU!

5

MEDIA MERCHANT?

Are you known for being a bit grumpy with the media?

✓ If Yes, you're Jose Mourinho!

✗ If No, go to question 6!

6

TRACKSUIT GAFFER?

Would you normally wear a tracksuit to matches?

✓ If Yes, you're Jurgen Klopp!

✗ If No, you're Pep Guardiola!

7

LONE STRIKERS?

Do you like to play with just one striker leading the line?

✓ If Yes, you're Nuno Espirito Santo!

✗ If No, you're Steve Bruce!

8

EPIC EXPERIENCE?

Do you think it's vital to have a lot of managerial experience?

✓ If Yes, go to question 9!

✗ If No, go to question 10!

9

TACTICAL MASTERCLASS INCOMING!

INTERNATIONAL?

Would you also like to manage an international side?

✓ If Yes, you're Marcelo Bielsa!

✗ If No, you're Carlo Ancelotti!

10

LONDON HAS LOTS OF DEADLY DERBIES!

LOCATION?

Would you prefer to manage a club based in London?

✓ If yes, you're Mikel Arteta!

✗ If no, you're Ole Gunnar Solskjaer!

PACKED EVERY ISSUE WITH...

MASSIVE STARS

RED-HOT GEAR

ACE INTERVIEWS

EPIC FEATURES

AMAZING POSTERS

PICS, QUIZZES & MORE!

SUBSCRIBE TO MATCH!...

CALL
01959 543 747
QUOTE: MATAN22

ONLINE
SHOP.KELSEY.
CO.UK/MATAN22

QUIZ ANSWERS!

Premier League Quiz — Pages 24-25

YouTube Star: Wilfried Zaha.

MATCH Maths: 3 + 5 = 8.

The Nickname Game: 1. D; 2. A; 3. B; 4. C.

Freaky Faces: Timo Werner.

Grounded: Molineux.

Footy Mis-MATCH: See right.

Prem Strikers Wordfit — Page 26

Champions League Quiz — Pages 38-39

Sport Switch: Kylian Mbappe.

Champions League Quiz:
1. True; 2. 13; 3. Arsenal; 4. Cristiano Ronaldo; 5. Krestovsky Stadium.

Close-Up: 1. Thomas Muller; 2. Mohamed Salah; 3. Neymar; 4. Marco Reus.

Soccer Scrabble: Ronaldinho.

Name The Team: 1. Antonio Rudiger; 2. Thiago Silva; 3. Edouard Mendy; 4. Kai Havertz; 5. Cesar Azpilicueta; 6. N'Golo Kante; 7. Reece James; 8. Ben Chilwell; 9. Jorginho; 10. Timo Werner.

Super Skippers: Juventus - Giorgio Chiellini; PSG - Marquinhos; Sevilla - Jesus Navas; Man. United - Harry Maguire.

Goal Machines:
1. Lille; 2. Bayern Munich; 3. Villarreal; 4. Liverpool; 5. Real Madrid; 6. Atalanta.

MATCH Winner: Kai Havertz.

Champions League Brain-Buster — Page 40

1. True; 2. Xavi; 3. Benfica; 4. 2017; 5. Borussia Dortmund; 6. Erling Haaland; 7. Four; 8. Cameroon; 9. Carlo Ancelotti; 10. Germany.

WSL Quiz — Pages 58-59

Camera Shy:
Laura Vetterlein, Lucy Bronze & Ella Toone.

Crazy Names: 1. Reading; 2. Arsenal; 3. Brighton; 4. Everton; 5. Leicester; 6. Man. United.

WSL Heroes: 1. C; 2. A; 3. B.

True or False?:
1. False; 2. False; 3. True; 4. False; 5. True.

Mystery Mascot: Chelsea.

Spot The Ball: G8.

Guess The Winners: 2021 - Chelsea; 2020 - Chelsea; 2019 - Arsenal; 2018 - Chelsea.

Derby Rivals: 1. B; 2. C; 3. A.

Crazy Kit: Everton.

WSL Wordsearch — Page 60

EFL Quiz — Pages 70-71

Job Swap: Matty Taylor.

Back To The Future: James Vaughan.

Club Sharers: Fulham.

Flipped: Lewis Grabban.

Camera Shy:
Lucas Joao, Lukas Jutkiewicz & Ovie Ejaria.

Nottingham Forest Quiz:
1. The City Ground; 2. True; 3. Scotland; 4. Derby County; 5. 29 years old.

Guess The Winners:
2021 - Hull; 2019 - Luton; 2018 - Wigan; 2017 - Sheffield United.

Spot The Sponsor: 1. Peterborough; 2. Sunderland; 3. Sheffield Wednesday; 4. West Brom; 5. Forest Green; 6. Cambridge.

MATCH Winner: Kenny Dougall.

EFL Crossword — Page 72

Across: 1. Ten; 4. Newcastle; 6. Crewe; 9. Nine; 12. Sheffield United; 13. Defender; 17. Nineteen; 18. Wales; 19. Lincoln; 20. Poland.

Down: 2. Nike; 3. French; 5. Sheffield Wednesday; 7. August; 8. Salford; 10. Derby; 11. Liverpool; 14. Wigan; 15. Right; 16. Chile.

Quiz Posters

Heung-Min Son Quiz:
1. True; 2. Bayer Leverkusen; 3. Burnley; 4. Europa League; 5. True.

Caroline Graham Hansen Quiz:
1. False; 2. Wolfsburg; 3. More than 80; 4. Italy; 5. Nike.

Karim Benzema Quiz:
1. False; 2. 2009; 3. Four; 4. Austria; 5. True.

Mason Mount Quiz:
1. True; 2. Six; 3. Derby; 4. Ukraine; 5. False.

Vivianne Miedema Quiz:
1. True; 2. 83; 3. Bayern Munich; 4. Ten; 5. True.

Zlatan Ibrahimovic Quiz:
1. Malmo; 2. Lyon; 3. Less than 20; 4. Taekwondo; 5. Real Madrid.

Virgil van Dijk Quiz:
1. Everton; 2. FA Cup; 3. Celtic; 4. True; 5. John Terry.

One point for each correct answer!

SCORE /236